Canine
Communication
The Language of a Species

Sally Gutteridge

Copyright

No part of this book may be reproduced in any form - written, electronic, recording, or photocopying without written permission of the publisher or author. The exception would be in the case of brief quotations embodied in the critical articles or reviews and pages where permission is specifically granted by the author.

Although every precaution has been taken to verify the accuracy of the information contained herein, the author and publisher assume no responsibility for any errors or omissions. No liability is assumed for damages that may result from the use of the information contained within.

Writer: Sally Gutteridge
Illustrator: Dayle Smith
Formatter: Sandeep Likhar
Editor: Rebecca Stranney

Books may be purchased by contacting
the publisher and author at:
info@sallygutteridge.com
www.sallygutteridge.com

Imprint: Independently published

Table of Contents

Special Thanks

A word of heartfelt thanks to the contributors of photographs for this book. Our canine guests and their humans.

Apollo	Hunter	Rory
Bailey	Jess	Sammy
Beau	Juno	Shiloh
Bella	Kobe	Sky
Brantley	Kusch	Skye
Buckley	Lexi	Sunny
Buddy	Lucy	Tali
Bugg	Lutza	Tilly
Caleb	Maggie	TJ
Darcy	Millie	Toby
Dixie	Milo	Zuka
Dobby	Molly	Otis
Doug	Ollie	Milo
Douglas	Queen Bea	Milo
Elsa	Rick	Lexi
Enzo	Rocky	Lucky
Gus	Rolo	

Gareth Brown Photographer.

Introduction

Canine communication is one of the most interesting things about our dogs. From their slightest to their most overt shapes, postures, tensions and movements, each telling us something about the way they feel.

Communication is information passed between two or more individuals to achieve an ultimate aim. It's based on how each individual feels and what information they want to share. For dogs, all of their behaviours are a natural reflection of their internal state and as the people responsible for their welfare it's our job to properly understand them, by learning how they communicate their feelings and intentions.

Whilst some communication attempts are obvious, others are subtle and easily misunderstood or even unnoticed. The purpose of my work here is to help you automatically understand how each dog you meet is communicating, what may be behind their specific behaviours and how to communicate efficiently and effectively back by using techniques that the dog is most likely to understand.

Along with written descriptions I use a variety of images in the book. We begin with illustrations to teach shapes and positions as effectively as possible.

We then move onto photographs, providing the detailed description and show you various formats of how the communication looks on the dog. The aim is not only to tell you what the dog's communication looks like and why, but to show you and help you recognise their language in the real world too. Some of the most important areas are covered in the first half of the book then reiterated later, simply because that will help you understand them better in real world scenarios.

This book will help you to understand not only your own dogs but also the communication attempts of every dog that you meet. When you start to properly and skilfully communicate with dogs it's a fascinating and heartening journey, that's fair on them and an amazing experience for us.

CHAPTER ONE

Individuality

"Many dogs can understand almost every word humans' say, while humans seldom learn to recognize more than half a dozen barks, if that. And barks are only a small part of the dog language. A wagging tail can mean so many things. Humans know that it means a dog is pleased, but not what a dog is saying about his pleasedness"
—Dodie Smith, 101 Dalmatians

Enlightened Observation

Enlightened observation is the act of observing from a point of neutrality and education. When we practice observing in this way, we avoid projecting our own experiences and beliefs onto dogs. The human mind is an excellent projector, think of a time you have argued with a partner or family member in the past. I bet you looked at them and assumed that you knew what they were thinking and how they felt – which fuelled your fire of annoyance. Arguments are usually based on a lack of excellent communication and assumptions, on projection as opposed to true understanding.

Projection leads to misinformation, which in the case of dogs means that we assume how they feel – rather than giving them the chance to tell us in the best way they can. The more neutral we can be when we observe dogs and the more education we have, the best chance they have of showing us how they are feeling. Assumptions, projections and the natural desire to rush in and interact with a dog, blinds us to their language and communications. Enlightened observation offers space, and postpones action – giving the dog a chance to tell us what he needs.

Here's a little challenge.

Observe yourself for a while, when out with your dog or interacting with a dog you meet. Do you dive in and touch or interact? Or do you wait for a few seconds, asking yourself what the dog in front of you is trying to say?

If you dive in, don't be too hard on yourself, it's our nature, we are descended from apes and our ancestors are grabbers and doers. The important thing to remember though is that dogs are descended from wolves and they are hesitant observers – which is where our communication styles clash. Dogs generally don't want to be touched, particularly not by strangers, as it's not really in their nature. A life of being touched without giving permission must be pretty tough too, dogs are tolerant animals, which is another reason why they truly are man's best friend.

When you become aware of being a doer it's easier to change your own behaviour and create a little space in your mind. That space can then be filled with observation, respect and proper communication.

Education

There are many types of canine education in the world today. Some are lagging behind and still think dogs are all aspiring alpha wolves, others believe that dogs are fair game to be punished and pronged whilst the rest of us believe in kindness. One thing we can all learn though, is dog language and enlightened communication. Because let's face it – nobody really knows how a dog feels, apart from that dog. It's almost all guesswork, but at least when we practice enlightened observation, we can make an educated guess.

A few generations ago canine education had little formal stance in the world. As humans we claimed expert status quickly and taught each other based on our opinions, what our dogs were thinking and feeling. Some still do that – which is a bit cringeworthy – but most people who teach about dogs now, tend to follow the science. Thankfully that science is fabulous and growing all the time. It has real heart and dogs are being studied for who they are, so projection is minimised, whilst we all learn about the dog's needs – directly from that dog.

The book you are reading is based on fundamental; science based knowledge and enlightened observation. I hope you learn a lot from it and that your relationship with your dog, and every dog you meet, benefits greatly.

What Makes an Individual?

Individuality is a term we can apply to all living creatures, not just humans. Often we only apply it to the ones we know and have learned about whilst caring for them. Yet individuality is applicable to every single animal and particularly those who reproduce via meiosis.

Meiosis is the meeting of DNA to produce offspring. DNA is the spice of life and creates biological individuality. A dog's DNA is split directly between half of his mother's and half of his father's. This naturally leads to the dog having a quarter of each of his grandparents' DNA. We can also refer to DNA as genetic influence, so a dog that is born to two black parents will likely be a black dog – yet if his grandparents were yellow, they may have an influence on the puppy's colour.

The domestic dog is a varied animal, thanks to artificial selection. When we joined company, he was likely a wild animal. Compared to the dogs of today he would have looked very much like one species. Now though, we have dogs bred for so many different roles that they all look different to each other and certainly only a small handful resemble his wild gray wolf cousin. Dogs look different to each other because of the genetic influence of artificial selection, some of the physical changes were purposeful and some were part of a different aim and just happened to come along for the ride.

Genetic influence is fascinating and can be addictive to learn about. Each gene has a job to do in the body. Artificial selection selects the genes that provide useful traits – so humans decide which dog is to be the father and mother of the puppies based on the traits of the parents. Depending on the final result required by the people involved, this can be focussed on physical, behavioural traits or both.

Genes can have ride-along genes. A litter of puppies may be bred to be tame and be easy companion dogs, but this can affect their appearance too. The same thing can happen the other way around. The dog who is bred to look a certain way can suffer with health issues created by their DNA and genetic inheritance. This happens not because illness has been created on purpose, but because someone has irresponsibly tried to breed dogs for appearance alone.

Genetic influence affects behaviour and body language in many ways. For communication purposes when looking at a dog of a specific breed, we have to consider their accents and ability to communicate via their physiology. We do this by learning about their neutrality – both of the dogs we know and love and those breeds that we meet occasionally too.

Learning about dogs already familiar to us is easier because we get to watch them all the time. We know how they respond to things and we can match their body language to those responses. Educating ourselves on other breeds is a good idea too, particularly if you work with dogs or plan to in the future, or if you simply want to understand dogs that you meet.

A Varied Appearance

Understanding dogs of various biological shapes and accents is paramount to understanding the species. Variety in the way a dog communicates occurs more than visually but vocally too. Dog breeds not only look and act slightly differently, but they also vocalise and hear signals differently, they probably also smell a bit different too.

For Example:

The Old English Sheepdog is bred with a round head and round eyes. He has long hair on his ears that keep them heavy and usually also has long hair on his face, which may disguise facial expressions.

If he meets another of his own breed they are likely to understand each other depending on their social skills.

Now if a Jack Russell meets an Old English Sheepdog he will see a face that shows little expression, covered in hair and complemented by ears that are too heavy to move much at all. If this is the first Old English Sheepdog this JRT has met, he may find the dog a little unnerving. Just as we would if another person communicates differently to us.

Dogs read meta-signals of communication. They look out for tiny cues of how the other dog is feeling and if those cues are hindered by a hairy face or inability to show eye shapes, it can cause confusion and even fear.

We must remember that a dog's physical appearance is individual to that dog. He might be long haired and experiencing hackles – where the hair on the back and neck stands up – but we might not be able to see them. He could even be showing his teeth but if we can't see them through the hair on his face, we could misread that dog's intention.

Similarly, vocalisations are breed and individual based. We can consider them the dog's accent. Some dogs growl a lot during play whilst others find that intimidating. Other dogs chat, for example the Rottweiler, whilst it can sound like growling it's used by this breed for all manner of happy communications too. The fact that different dogs are so vocally varied makes an excellent case for observing everything in context and reading the situation and body language of the dog – rather than assuming you know the reason for the growl.

One of my Jack Russells (Chips) growls a lot, the other (Vinny) only growls if he means it or is playing with his housemate. When Chips meets other dogs that he likes and wants to play with, he growls, play bows and wags. It's confusing for the other dog and often their person looks shocked too, but Chips means no harm and is asking to play in the way that he does at home. It's how he has learned to communicate.

Cosmetic and Genetic Alterations

Genetic alterations are carried out based on Kennel Club guidelines of how dogs should look. For example, the English bulldog with his heavy stance and flat face, snorting as he walks because of flattened airways can be terrifying to a dog who hasn't met him before.

Without the aid of a tail for communication, when it has been removed via cosmetic surgery, and with the appearance of posturing this dog can be like an alien to other dogs.

Cosmetic alterations thankfully are becoming less common than they used to be. The most common of them include docked tails and pinned ears, both of which are unnecessary procedures that cause pain initially and take away a substantive part of a dog's communication repertoire. Veterinary professionals are speaking out against cosmetic surgery for dogs. One day we might be able to influence genetic alterations in the same way. Carrying them out only to make the dogs healthier rather than to meet a standard of appearance designed for the human eye, I do hope so.

Individuality through Learning

The first few months of a dog's life are filled with brain growth and development. They are learning about the world they live in and the other animals they share it with.

If a puppy learns from people and other animals that are excellent communicators, they are likely to become excellent communicators themselves. If they are isolated from other dogs for their first few months, they will be scared of and awkward with other dogs. There's a well-known experiment carried out by Scott and Fuller that took a puppy from a litter and completely isolated him for a few months. When the puppy returned to his siblings he didn't recognise them – not only as his siblings but also as his own species. This is a horrible experiment, and thankfully science has moved on. We can see why though, that a dog taken from his litter and not socialised with other dogs in effective, positive ways, will likely suffer socially.

Individuality through learning can take many forms. A dog who grows up with another dog is likely to learn the other dog's habits. A dog who is ignored when he shows polite requests, will probably cease the requests because they don't work. A dog that grows up being punished by humans is likely to fear humans and communicate towards us a great deal differently than a dog who hasn't learned to fear us at all.

When we communicate with any dog, in fact any animal at all – even humans, we must first acknowledge them as an individual with their own biology, feelings, learning experiences and beliefs to have the best possible chance of understanding them and their own communication.

Communication Types

As we already know, exactly how dogs communicate is part learned and in part genetic. Skilled communication is one of the best things we can teach a dog when we live or work with them. Teaching ourselves to step back and truly understand how a dog is communicating, along with what he's saying is of great importance.

Whilst humans communicate with a lot of visual and verbal efforts, and a few barely noticeable meta signals, dogs do the same but add a lot of skill through their olfactory system too.

Scent

Dogs have amazing noses, whilst we walk into an area and see the picture of that area through our eyes, the dog will walk into the area and *see* the picture directly through scent.

If we were to drop a small bit of tasty food in long grass in a relatively small area, the dog will smell that food through its scent particles and find it immediately. Dogs that like to roll in nasty things can detect something that they consider delicious, from metres away. Giving them the rolling edge well before we can get near and prevent the distressing shoulder dip and delighted poop dance.

The same sense of smell will enable dogs to identify us before they recognise us by sight. I recently saw a video where a man had been in hospital for a long time and his dog walked up to him, a little worried. Even though the dog could see his human he only recognised the person he loved when he smelled him, then the wriggly delighted greeting began. Scent can enable dogs to communicate across the gap of time too. A dog might urinate on a lamppost, then later another dog will smell that urine and know much about the first dog.

The dog's anal glands also hold much information. The anal glands are two little sacs of fluid on the dog's anus. They are the reason dogs sniff each other's rear ends when greeting. Whilst people may find it a little odd, greeting via the rear is perfectly normal and much politer in dog speak than greeting a stranger face to face. If we consider the anal gland an identity card, we can see exactly how and why dogs go straight to the point of most information when saying hello.

The two dogs in this picture show a well-mannered curved greeting, although both their tails are quite high showing that they are both confident to greet, without fear or anxiety.

Sight

Dogs communicate visually in a similar way to people. When a dog is approached by an unknown dog they will assess everything from the other dog's eye shape, ear position, posture, movement types, tail and facial expression. They may not consciously consider every part of the other dog's approach - just as we don't when an unknown person approaches us – but they will assess quickly and prepare for whatever the other dog's visual appearance is telling them.

A lot of what a dog sees when an unknown dog approaches can be missed easily by the human eye. Subtle shapes and tiny changes become an overall appearance to us, yet to the dog being approached provide a vast amount of information.

An example of this is how my boy Chips reacted to an off lead Jack Russell a few months ago. Chips is a fearful dog and like many terriers has adopted attack as a form of defence. He never attacks and wouldn't fight but he will warn a dog off if he's scared. The other dog approached our group silently when we were out walking and within a second of seeing her Chips moved away, showing none of his usual outspoken greeting. The other dog then attacked our smallest member severely, with no sound and much determination. The whole thing was extremely distressing for all of us, but particularly for our tiny Yorkie. Yet, Chips knew exactly what the other dog was capable of from the moment he saw her and took a wise detour from both her and his usual response.

The initial visual assessment takes place quickly before communication begins. A dog that tends to show anxiety based defensiveness on the lead may jump, growl and bark towards a passing dog. A well-socialised other dog will usually just walk on by. A dog that has not learned to communicate or read the signals of others may approach anyway and offer his own form of inept communication usually bouncing around, whilst a dog that has learned to be aggressive to others may even approach the on lead defensive (anxious) dog to attack him.

When a meeting between two well-balanced dogs goes well there are still many signals, but they are based on assessment that becomes co-operation. Try to imagine a successful greeting as a dance, the dogs see each other and swap tiny signals until they actually meet. The exact signals are based in body language, shapes and expressions. They may even include vocalisations.

Sound

Common sound based canine communication includes growling, barking and whining but there are many more. A socially competent dog will not usually greet another via barking. They may offer a warning growl or a whine of excitement, but barking and howling is usually saved for communication at distance.

The dog who has learned to be scared of others may bark and growl at them, telling them to stay away. They may also use the same overt communication style to tell people, children, cars, bikes and any other scary thing to stay away. Most times this is successful for them – because no-one sane wants to approach an aggressive looking dog – so the dog learns that the behaviour works and it becomes a habit.

Sometimes people find vocal communication from dogs inconvenient or annoying, so they punish or attempt to stop it. This is a mistake and is very unfair on the dog. If you have ever been subjected to a one sided conversation, where you couldn't get a word in and were just talked at or pushed by someone who seemed unable to listen, you will understand how this can feel. Imagine now that everyone you meet did that to you. You would soon get fed up and may even lose your temper simply because you think it's the only way to be heard.

When a dog makes a sound it's a communication. It may be based on a habit that is not completely healthy, for example feeling the need to guard something or chase something scary away, but it's still precious communication. When this communication itself is considered a problem, without the reasons behind it being explored, we are walking on shaky ground.

In a world where dog training and behaviour lacks sufficient regulation, punishment is still regularly used to change behaviour by poor quality dog trainers. Unfortunately, this can lead to a situation where a dog trying to communicate his inner feelings is punished for the sound based communication with no understanding of why it's occurring. This leads to a dog who feels unable to communicate for fear of punishment, so he supresses his attempts because not only do they not work, but they also result in something unpleasant or painful.

The most efficient way to receive sound based communication is to listen and receive it, then ask yourself why it's happening along with what the dog is telling you. Then if it becomes problematic or seems unhealthy for the dog, work out how to change the behaviour via environmental assessment and science-based behaviour modification.

Whilst we are not creating a behaviour modification learning experience here, let's just take a brief look at common vocal communications and what the feelings behind them may be. The following are generic scenarios and I urge you to seek professional advice from a suitably qualified canine specialist if your dog shows these behaviours. My descriptions are provided purely to enhance understanding.

1. Growling over the food bowl or a treat is based not in true aggression but the fear of losing the resource. If this was punished, or the food was taken anyway the dog has learned that he will lose the food so next time will be even more tense. If the dog gets the safe space he's entitled to, whilst he eats his food or treat, he will become more relaxed whilst he eats and less likely to growl because he knows he can eat in peace. Finally, if the dog learns that resources are plentiful and never get taken away, he will become so relaxed around them that the growling may stop altogether.

2. Barking at dogs on the lead when out walking is a common default behaviour of the fearful dog. Whilst this may be inconvenient it's still precious communication. The barking dog is simply trying to maintain a space he feels safe in, by chasing the other dog away via a seemingly aggressive display. If we go closer to the other dog, our own will bark harder. If we move away from the other dog, our own will start to relax because his safe space is being naturally increased. Fundamentally here, the dog is barking for space and if we were to continue towards the other dog we'd be punishing our own dog's communication. They'd likely become more distressed as the distance decreased and their trust in us may diminish.

When a dog has learned not to communicate at the hands of someone who didn't properly understand him, he may stop doing it. Yet if you respond to it with observation and respect, following it with effective communication of your own the dog will learn that it works and feel safe enough to communicate his needs and feelings to you.

Touch

Touch between dogs is usually limited to familiarity or fighting. Unlike people who like to shake hands, even hug strangers, dogs are careful about who they touch and why. Familiarity is an excellent reason that dogs touch each other, which is linked to their individual preference of social distance.

Like people some dogs are quite tactile and others less. Generally, dogs are touched by people much more than they would like to be. We should always ask permission before we touch them and respectfully adhere to the signals they offer in response. In some cases, a new and anxious dog that joins a human home will learn to ask for touch - eventually enjoying it – yet whether we touch a dog or not should always be dog led and not just because we want to.

Similarly, how we touch dogs may need to be re-assessed. Anything coming over their head or a hand pushed in their face for a sniff is literally "in your face" and if we consider that dogs greet differently, we realise that going towards one with our hand outstretched into their face is neither wise or respectful. The golden rule really is, wait at a distance and avoid eye contact and if the dog wants to come to you – then reciprocate his greeting in kind.

Dogs may or may not enjoy touch with others. Some are precious about their personal space whilst others all pile into one bed leaving the rest of them empty. It's lovely to see our dogs cuddled up together but we can't force it. We must allow them to be themselves.

Play between dogs most often involves touching in some way. They may wrestle, muzzle fence or bash each other with front paws. Play is a number of behaviours left over from the dog's predator ancestors and occurs simply for fun, bonding and sometimes to communicate a bigger message. We will talk more about play later in the book.

Takeaway Points

- As humans we want to immediately interact with any dog we meet. Socially competent dogs tend to stand back and assess a situation before interaction and usually would prefer we did the same.

- Every dog is an individual.

- All dogs have *accents* based on their physiology and breed type.

- Excellent communication is learned by positive social experiences with other excellent communicators.

- A dog that is isolated from other dogs for the first few months of his life will suffer fear or anxiety when re-introduced to them.

- Dogs communicate predominantly through scent.

- Sight, sound and touch are also part of the dog's communication repertoire.

- Vocal communication should be respected as the dog trying to tell us something and never be punished. If vocalisations such as excessive barking become problematic they can be modified via science based coaching but only when we know exactly why the dog is barking and the coaching deals with his inner state too.

- Most dogs are touched by people more than they would like to be.

- We can learn to respect dogs by reading their communication attempts and knowing when they want to be touched, then respect their space when they don't.

CHAPTER TWO

Body Language

"Science has so far been unable to tell us how self-aware dogs are, much less whether they have anything like our conscious thoughts. This is not surprising, since neither scientists nor philosophers can agree about what the consciousness of humans consists of, let alone that of animals."
—John Bradshaw

Body language is communication telling us how the dog feels. Canine body language is a range of signals that combine to tell us the dog's internal state and what exactly he is trying to tell us. To fully understand the body language that we are going to explore here, it's important to know a little about stress and how it affects the dog's behaviour from the inside out.

Taking two forms, stress can be useful in short bursts for learning or achieving peak performance. Think about a time you had an important task to complete and performed better than you ever have before, to achieve a specific aim. This type of stress is called eustress and is an excellent learning boost for people and dogs.

Imagine now that the task was too big for you to achieve, even with the presence of eustress, or something was way too scary for you to cope with. When we are overwhelmed we go beyond eustress into distress and so do our dogs.

The dog's ability to cope with stress will move from eustress to distress based on his own capacity for coping. As he enters distress we can consider he has gone beyond his coping threshold and this is where his survival instinct kicks in and stress becomes damaging enough to affect the immune system, digestive system and hormones in the body.

Stress is a response of the dog's nervous system which is based purely on keeping the dog alive and safe. It's an inner process that the dog will have no control over. Stress applies to all animals and all people, in fact anyone with a central nervous system will experience stress because it's our natural survival switch.

The thing that makes a dog stressed is commonly known as a trigger, the stress trigger switches on the stress reaction and the dog experiences an influx of adrenaline (body stress chemical) and cortisol (brain stress chemical) in preparation to fight or take flight. There are a couple of other choices that it's possible to make when stressed, they include fooling around or freezing. Each of these choices look different in the dog:

- Flight is where the dog chooses to leave the situation and prevent any kind of fight. Flight is often rare now in the domestic dog because we have them on the lead or they are prevented from taking flight in other ways, plus many dogs have learned that fight related behaviour seems to work for them. Flight may not manifest as running hellbent in another direction, it could be something as simple as being off lead so going around an approaching dog in a healthy curve, to avoid any possible confrontation.

- Fight is where the dog chooses to face his fears head on. When this occurs in wild animals it's perfectly natural but in the case of domestic dogs we often unknowingly place them in a position where they feel they have no choice but to fight. Something simple like walking towards another dog – with our own dog on the lead - on a forest trail can stress a worried dog enough to leave them believing they can't escape, so they display fight behaviour. It's simply because they are stressed by the other dog, who is their trigger and they can't help it. However, how many times have you seen a dog blamed and punished for this kind of behaviour, I expect it's quite a few.

- Fooling around is the third active response to stress. It can manifest as height seeking, hand nipping and general animation. Sometimes, stress based fooling around looks like play but it doesn't have the same relaxed stance as play, the dog looks tenser and desperate when he's in this state.

- Freeze is most often practiced by animals that are prey as opposed to predator. For example, if a rabbit in a field sees a fox approaching his entire body will freeze in the hope that lack of movement will result in him not being seen. Domestic dogs are now neither predator or prey, but they can freeze and hope that a threat goes away, like the rabbit. The dog who suffers from learned helplessness is most likely to freeze because they have learned that no effort takes them to safety, so they just wait it out.

Learned Helplessness

Learned helplessness is ironically linked to the name directly associated with positive psychology in people, Martin Seligman. Whilst carrying out an experiment on dogs, to attempt understanding of human depression, he discovered that putting dogs in painful circumstances can lead to them not trying to escape when the trigger for pain stops. He did this by administering a series of electric shocks to dogs that couldn't escape - then administering shocks to the same dogs that could escape - but the dogs by then had learned helplessness so didn't try. It then took much longer for the dogs involved to realise that they had regained control over their fate.

The type of testing that Seligman was doing is coined comparative psychology; where the animal is tested and associated with the human brain and thinking patterns, it happens with many animals even today. The experiment was unkind and unfair to the dogs but thankfully ethology is now leading the way with canine research.

Domestic dogs can experience learned helplessness if they have been in a position where they have no choices, been abused or hurt by people. For example, puppy farm dogs, who have spent a lot of time abused and known no kindness may appear helpless if they escape into a kind home. Dogs that have been exposed to unethical training methods such as electric shocks, prong collars or brute force and ignorance will start to emotionally shut down and may reach a state of learned helplessness if their circumstances don't change for the better.

Learned helplessness can be undone. Depending on how long the dog suffered it may take weeks, months or even years. It took my little Yorkie two years in a safe, loving and respectful home environment to recover from six years being bred from in a puppy farm, when she realised she was safe she started to sparkle and hasn't stopped since. It could take a dog that has been briefly trained with force and fear, then wisely moved to an educated and kind trainer, a lot less time to recover. As always, dogs are individuals with personal healing time.

Reflections of an Inner State

Try to imagine that a dog shows us exactly how he feels on the inside, often about what is happening on the outside at the time. A dog that is in a calm, neutral environment will reflect that in his body language. If something scary or stressful happens it will change the way that dog feels inside so it will change how he looks. Similarly, if something pleasing or exciting happens the dog will feel pleased or excited and display that, for us all to see.

Everything is linked just like in the image below. So, if you are observing a dog and see a behaviour change, follow their line of sight, to the trigger, and back to the dog's body language change, to empower you to explore the dogs changed emotional state.

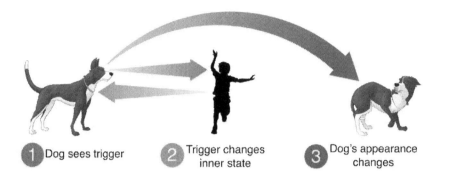

1 Dog sees trigger 2 Trigger changes inner state 3 Dog's appearance changes

Important Note

Not all changes are triggered by something on the outside of the dog. Some may start on the inside environment. For example, the dog may be in pain so his behaviour changes, he could be showing signs of Canine Cognitive Dysfunction which changes behaviour through brain degeneration or his diet might affect how he feels. It's vital to consider all these things too and if you haven't already read it, my book Inspiring Resilience in Fearful and Reactive Dogs goes into much more detail on these points. Plus of course if there is any doubt on the wellbeing or health of a dog, the first stop must always be the veterinarian.

Shapes and Expressions

The basis of body language, before we assess movement, is shapes and expressions. For example, the eye shape, ear shape, facial expression and body position, including posture, all tell us something about the dog.

It's surprising how many people can't read the most basic requests of their dogs, or maybe understand their own but crowd strange dogs with an assumption that they are keen to interact. Often the dog wants nothing less than to be patted on the head by a determined strange human. People often try and touch our tiny Yorkie because she's extremely cute, but she is so scared that we work hard to keep her out of reach. The world is full of fly by patters.

Observing in context is an important part of understanding our dogs. For example, a dog may appear tense but as an invitation to play, or he may bow in a position that resembles the play bow, but actually be asking for space. Looking at not only the whole dog but also the environment at the exact time of the communication and behaviour he is showing.

When we can read shapes and expressions we are more likely to understand every dog we meet. It's a good idea to learn the neutral position of dogs you have contact with regularly and certainly your own dogs. A neutral position is best described as a relaxed dog, or as much as possible, the absence of any strong emotion. When he's not, excited, worried or scared – how does your dog look? When you're not interacting, reacting or playing, how do his ears, eyes, posture or tail look. That's most likely to be his neutral position. From there, when emotions are experienced, that's when a dog goes from neutral to a reaction based stance. The reaction, whether happy or not, is based on whatever is going on in the environment at the time.

If you work with dogs I suggest you learn a bit about the neutral position of a few of the common breeds you work with, this will give you an edge when observing them and understanding how they feel.

Ears

Individuality dictates the shape of ears and the dog's ability to move them. Yet communication through ears is based on the same physiological movement regardless of ear shape. It's just that we only see what the dog's physiology will allow.

The predominant role of a dog's ears is to listen. This can be intertwined with communication or linked to an ancient need to be safe and avoid danger. Listening is achieved by all dogs by opening the gap into to ear as effectively as possible. If the ears are naturally pricked, this is easy, for heavy, hairy ears in breeds such as the spaniel this is more difficult but remember – the attempt at movement is the same but biology makes it appear different.

Listening dogs will direct their ears towards a sound they are focussing on. Sometimes directing the ears in two completely different directions, this may be subtle but watch out for it and you will notice it.

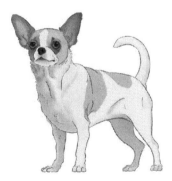

Alertness is shown by ears being pulled forward and pricked towards the object of the dog's attention. This is obvious when a dog's ears are naturally pricked anyway as the ears will be pulled forward on the dog's head as if he's trying to point them towards the object of his interest.

All dogs will try that but for some their anatomy simply won't allow it.

When a dog feels conflicted his ears will naturally stick out each side of his head - as much as his biology will allow. This is commonly known as airplane ears and shows us that the dog has two or more conflicting feelings about the environment or who he is interacting with. We often see this type of ear shape from a dog who is uneasy about a meeting with another, but enjoying it a little bit too.

The ear position of appeasement is ears held high and towards the back of the head. Appeasement behaviour aims to avoid and defuse tension and you may see this when your dog meets another on a walk, and offers a peaceful greeting. High ears are only possible for some breed types, but all dogs will try.

When a dog is scared they will pull their ears towards the back of their head. The further back the dog's ears go, the more fearful he is. To the point that some types of ear many actually lay flat and seem to disappear, in a position known as seal ears. If a dog shows seal ears he will be extremely fearful. The dog in the picture below also has dilated pupils, another sign of severe anxiety.

When dogs who don't have the physiological ability to create seal ears are scared, their bodies will still try. Long eared dogs will attempt to pull their ears back, resulting in a pinched ear effect at the sides of their face. Don't be tempted to assume a dog is not scared because their ears don't show it, but other parts of their body do. They may not have the physical ability to create a seal ear appearance, but they may still be very scared.

Eyes

There's a saying that a dog's eyes are the window to his soul. Whilst this may be true, they are also a window to exactly how he feels at the time. We can see stress, fear, happiness and relaxation through the eyes of any dog, we just need to know what we are looking for. A happy and relaxed dog will show soft eyes. A relaxed or excited facial position and ears will accompany soft eyes.

Eye contact in general is avoided by dogs unless they are familiar and bonded with the person they share it with. When we know and love our dogs we can often sit and stare at each other happily. Interestingly to do this releases oxytocin which is a bonding hormone, usually shared between mother and baby but people and dogs experience it too, when we love each other.

If a dog experiences the stress reaction that we explored earlier, the pupils will dilate. This is an unconscious reaction but indicative of a change in the dog's inner state. Dilated pupils are an outward sign that the stress reaction has begun. This occurs with eustress and distress.

Whale eye describes the flash of white around a dog's eye when the animal is either stressed or threatening. This effect is caused by facial tension, the muscles in the face area become so tense that the whites of the eyes are shown. The dog below shows seal ears, whale eye and a general intention of appeasement. He also has a dipped head, which is another sign of deference.

Hard eyes and a hard stare are indication of focus or tension. If a dog meets another dog and stares intently at them with tension in their face and body, their own intention may be sinister. It's not advisable to allow a dog to stare or try to make eye contact with another dog, as a hard stare can escalate quickly into an attack. A confident dog with a hard stare is a worrying combination, as he usually means business.

Whilst socially intelligent people use eye contact to build trust and rapport with newly encountered people, not too little and not too much, it's advisable not to do that with unknown dogs. Unsolicited eye contact can make dogs uneasy as it will appear like confrontation or even a challenge.

When I first brought my Jack Russell Vinny home many years ago he was a poorly socialised and sensitive soul. He was on classifieds as free to good home and his current guardian couldn't keep him due to his, chaotic crocodile like tendencies. In the first instance she visited with him and the moment I looked in his eyes he launched into spook barking at me. My catchphrase after he moved in for good was "don't look in his eyes." He's twelve now and has been an amazing companion for his entire life. Yet I'm sure if anyone new looked in his eyes, he would still give them a good telling, his bark has a deafening pitch too.

Facial Muscles

A dog's facial expression includes a lot of subtlety. Everything from a slight eye shape change to the stretch of a lip will tell us something about how the dog feels. A facial expression can show relaxation or tension, excitement or happiness, just as the human face can. A dog's face shape determines their facial anatomy, but only to an extent. Generally speaking the dog with a relaxed face appears softer. The ears are in a neutral or interested position, eyes are soft or interested, there is no tension in the lips or whiskers and the facial muscles are soft. The dog below is showing relaxed facial features with a big smile.

A dog that is tense will show a harder facial expression. The lips may pull back and facial muscles will become tight. This dog may show a hard stare, they may pant, and the nostrils are likely to flare whilst they gather information from any available scent.

Moving between a relaxed face and a tense one can be subtle or quick depending on the trigger and how severe it is. A dog will not be totally relaxed, only to become suddenly very tense unless something particularly scary or worrying happens in the environment.

Lips

One of the subtler signs of tension and change of inner state are the dog's lips. Whilst lifting the lips to show the teeth is an obvious change, the lips pulled back when a dog is worried is also a big telling sign of tension. The dog in the picture below shows tense lips, avoidance of eye contact and seal ears. All telling us that he's uncomfortable and trying to avoid conflict.

Dogs purposely display their teeth for a few reasons and in a few different ways. They may be playing, or they could be issuing a warning. Teeth are a dog's true weapon to defend himself, if he ever needed to. The act of flashing their teeth is an excellent way for the dog to communicate that they have weapons, don't want to use them but are prepared to anyway. The dog in the picture below, showing his teeth is obviously uncomfortable. He is trying hard to avoid conflict and you would most likely see this body shape and communication from a dog that is asking to be left alone.

If you ever see a dog in the position above your greatest tool is distance. All he wants is space and when he gets the space he so desperately needs this dog's behaviour will settle down. No dog should be pushed to feeling like the one above does. Whilst on the rare occasion of an emergency it may be necessary not to back away, if at all possible space is all this dog wants. The less crowded he feels, the less likely this dog is to actually bite.

A dog showing a threat not triggered by immediate fear will behave much more confidently. He will square up and try for eye contact issuing a direct threat through a hard stare. This mouth position is also used in greeting and play, but usually without the hard stare and heavy tension around the face, which transforms this dog's mouth position into a confident threat.

This dog may not make much noise, a deep, low growl if any at all. Generally speaking the more noise that a dog makes, the less confident he is. The dog below shows a gaping mouth, showing all his teeth, a tense face and direct stare. This dog means it and is not simply asking for space by this point. Nonetheless backing off quietly, avoiding eye contact and not running is still highly advisable.

There are many differences between aggression shown through fear triggered by close proximity of a trigger and aggression for other reasons. It's wise to remember the context of a behaviour and the rest of the dog's body language. It doesn't make sense for a dog to do battle because he needs to maintain his long term survival. Just like wolves, the species is generally peaceful and will usually only aggress if pushed to.

There are exceptions though inclusive of genetic, learned and biological triggered aggression. Some dogs don't follow the typical peace maintenance lifestyle. They may be ill, have genetic influence that leads them to aggress, be taking medication that triggers outbursts or have learned it was their only choice early in their life. For aggression that seems to arise from nowhere, it's vital that the dog sees a vet first then a clinical or qualified, kind behaviour specialist.

Posture

As we move to the bigger picture we must add everything we have covered so far, the dog's ears, eyes and facial expression to the posture, which is great because we can get a much better idea of how the dog feels if we assess the whole dog.

Again, remember that every change of the dog's outside appearance gives us an idea of their inner state. Posture and tail position will be neutral when the dog feels neutral because there's nothing much happening in his environment. Every dog's neutral state is unique to him but will be similar to dogs of the same breed and type. For example, a Staffordshire Bull Terrier is naturally muscular even when he's so relaxed he could fall over, but if a Golden Retriever appeared with that same muscular stance he is likely to be very tense indeed.

A neutral dog is loose, relaxed and usually shows no tension in their face or body. The tail is at a relaxed position for that dog. For example, a whippet's tail will be tucked between his back legs whilst a Spitz will have it hooked high over his back. Take some time to observe your own dog's neutral position, that way you will be able to see when his inner state changes. If you work with dog's it's a great idea to get to know the neutral position of as many breed types as possible.

The way that a dog's posture changes is indicative of how he feels. A dog that shifts from neutral to happy and relaxed will become looser, if he gets excited he may wriggle wagging his tail and even his body. An easy way to remember this is by acknowledging that muscles fill up with tension when the stress reaction occurs. Whereas there is no need for tension when the dog is relaxed and happy, so the movement is loose and fluid. The muscles are still doing their job for movement, but they are not hindered by the potential need to fight or take flight.

When a stress reaction begins it can be associated with fear, anxiety, fright or any other distressing trigger (inclusive of a sudden pain). The dog will slow down as the muscle movement becomes less fluid and his body language will change. In this picture something has caught the dog's attention. He is looking at something in the distance and his tail has risen. There is neither fear, or animosity in this stare at the moment. His stance shows interest and from this point his inner state could go either way.

If the dog sees the trigger as a threat and is confident he may emotionally *"square up"* by keeping his eye on the trigger, tensing further and presenting a hard stare. His pupils will dilate as the stress reaction flows through his body. A raised tail tells us that he is aroused, confident or both. His hackles may raise, which act like our own goose bumps.

It is at this point where dogs that are considered reactive may begin to bark and appear as loud, scary and defensive as possible. Usually when they are on the lead this will be their default reaction to something scary. Volume goes up the less confident the dog is, they are literally trying to scare the trigger away through sound and visual threats because they can't cope with the possibility of an actual confrontation.

A silent, focussed dog is usually far more confident to follow through with aggression than a worried dog that is shouting from the rooftops how scary he is. Much of the time a lead adds to the reactive behaviour and if the dog were to be let off the lead when in close proximity to a trigger – despite his reactive display – he may just choose to run the other way. Don't try this at home though, just in case.

The other reaction a dog might show to a trigger is obvious fear. Whilst confidence and displays of aggression (true or not) make the dog appear taller and tenser, fear makes them appear smaller and tucked.

The dog in the image below has lowered his hind quarters and his tail is dropped. He shows facial tension, whale eye and seal ears. He lifts one paw which is this position is a sign that he's uneasy. Something has triggered a fear reaction in this dog and he's very worried indeed.

The more scared a dog becomes the lower he will tuck himself. If he's crowded he may resort to a warning and even a bite. The exception to that is learned helplessness, where the dog will just freeze and wait out whatever is going to happen to him. Again, if a dog that you are speaking to appears like either of the dogs above, they predominantly need space from the trigger, even if that trigger is you.

Tail

The dog's tail shows us much about how he feels. The following images give a broad idea of what wags mean but it's important to remember that every dog's tail has a neutral position, if it goes upwards the dog is confident and/or aroused whilst if it lowers the dog is unsure or scared. I highly recommend you do some tail watching, it's really interesting how even the smallest movements display a feeling or attempt at communication.

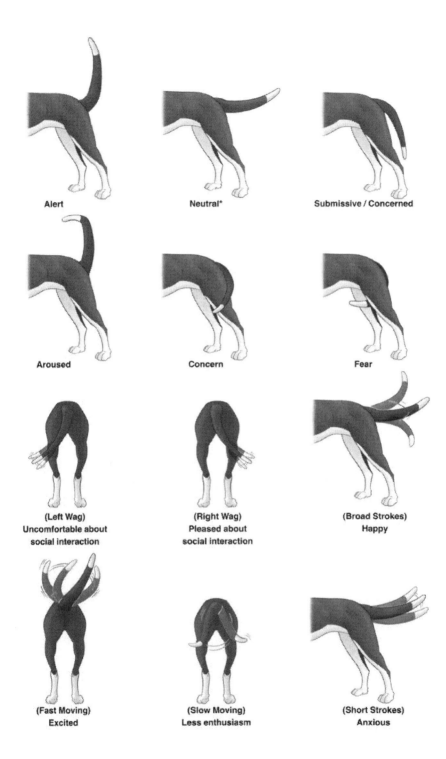

Takeaway Points

- All dogs have a neutral position.
- By familiarising ourselves with the neutral position of all areas of the dog's body individually and as a whole, we can read changes in the dog's emotional state.
- Stress is outside the dog's control.
- Stress triggers are individual for each dog.
- The external appearance of a dog is based on changes to their internal state.
- Stress makes a dog tense and relaxation makes him loose.
- Confidence makes a dog appear taller whilst fear makes him appear smaller and tucked in.
- All observations must consider the whole dog and the environment he is in.

CHAPTER THREE

Movement

I used to look at Smokey and think, "If you were a little smarter you could tell me what you were thinking," and he'd look at me like he was saying, "If you were a little smarter, I wouldn't have to." —Fred Jungclaus

With a good idea of shapes and postures by this point, we can begin looking at the signs that a dog's inner state is changing and there are many. Interestingly for us and unfortunately for dogs, relatively few people know the smaller signals which become bigger signals when they don't work. Often people only realise that there's something going on with a dog when they seemingly start acting overtly, however within a dog's natural capacity for communication much happens before that point.

Imagine that you and I were having a conversation and I was talking over you, loud and determined to give you my point of view. You may start getting fed up and glance away from me as a hint, maybe looking at your watch, you might stifle a yawn because you would really rather be somewhere, anywhere, else. Imagine though that my social skills are so awful that I miss all the polite movements you make and just keep talking. You might say something politely, but I ignore that too. I'm just not listening to your discomfort in the situation, I don't even seem to take a breath.

If you're anything like I *actually* am in that situation you would eventually burst a bit and leave. The situation eventually overrides any learned politeness and getting away is the only thing that matters. Now if you're put in that situation time and again, for example a coffee invitation from an enthusiastic chattering neighbour you will start to avoid the circumstance altogether. But what if you couldn't? What if you had to be in that situation three times a week indefinitely – what would you do? I suspect you would eventually realise that your attempts at counteracting the onslaught of chatter didn't work, so stop bothering. One day you might be feeling a little low; grouchy or fed up and it might all come out in a burst of emotion after building up for some time, wrecking the relationship and leaving the socially incompetent chatterer confused.

When we don't observe our dogs polite, small signals that something is going on for them, we are acting very much like the unaware chattering neighbour. We are putting them into a position where they are trying to tell us something in subtle, polite dog language and literally being ignored.

This situation repeated over and over again breaks down bonds, causes mistrust and leaves our dogs floundering with no other choices than to become louder and more obvious. This is why the dog "bit out of nowhere" after he has been "happily" fiddled with by a young child many times before. The truth is, he probably wasn't happy, it's just that no-one was listening.

Here's a warning. If this book is your first introduction to the subtleties of canine communication, your life will never be the same. You will see dogs everywhere you go, trying to communicate and being ignored. You will look at the "cute" videos online and inwardly cringe. This knowledge will change your experience of the world and every dog in it.

It's worth it though because you will be adding another language to your repertoire, the language of dog and there's nothing more wonderful than seeing a dog's eyes light up when he realises that you actually, truly understand him and can communicate back in a way that he understands too.

There's something else that's important to remember before we explore the communication signals. A dog will always learn to do what works for him. A dog that comes into your life as an adult may have tried all the smaller communications so many times and been ignored, that he has given up on them. So, he might not seem to show the smaller communication attempts at all – jumping directly to barking, growing or even snapping. The second possibility is the risk of shutdown or learned helplessness. So, the dog doesn't get louder when he's worried, he just freezes and offers no communication attempts at all. Both of these scenarios can occur if a dog has been ignored and traumatised in some way.

Imagine that communication is a process that begins small and increases in intensity until the dog is showing overtly that he's unhappy or needs something in the environment to change. When he lives with excellent communicators the process stays intact, because the earlier signals work. If he lives with poor communicators the process breaks, after practicing a few times, the dog learns that one specific choice of communication works and with practice that becomes his only choice. So, if a cut off signal of (for example looking away) works to stop another party approaching, great the dog knows that the other party is listening and honouring their request. If showing his teeth is the only thing that makes the other party back off and he practices this a few times, this will become his default response and all earlier signals become redundant.

The following images and descriptions begin subtle and become more overt. The early ones are small movements that can easily be missed if you're not looking. They show us the escalation of anxiety and stress in a dog that is experiencing something he is uncomfortable with, in progressive steps.

Signs of Emotional Discomfort

Every internal stress reaction begins with emotional discomfort. Remember the trigger, changing the internal state? It is at the very point the internal state begins to change that we see early signs of emotional discomfort in our dogs.

Glancing Away

Glancing away from a trigger then back to it is a sign that the dog may become a bit worried by it. This is often displayed when the trigger is at a safe distance and is also a cut-off signal to anyone approaching. If two well-balanced dogs meet and the first glances away, the second dog will usually heed their request and not approach. A glance away is literally a polite signal that the dog doesn't really want to interact. It's a subtle sign often missed by people who march up to pat an unknown dog on the head.

Licking

Licking the nose or lips is a telling sign that the dog feels uncomfortable. It may be extremely subtle to begin with, a little tongue flick that takes place in a split second, but the longer the situation goes on, without change the more overt the licking becomes. A big, slow and wide tongue shows us that the dog is feeling pretty uncomfortable.

Yawning

Yawning is another sign that the dog is beginning to feel uncomfortable. No-one knows the scientific reason for a yawn, for dogs or people. But we know when it happens, through tiredness and anxiety. If a dog yawns and it's not a place where he is relaxing or around sleeping, then it could be the onset of anxiety.

Staring

If glancing away hasn't worked and a trigger for the dog's stress continues to advance the dog may change his focus and stare directly at the thing which is worrying him. Some dogs sit when they do this, as a further signal that they want to keep things nice and calm. This behaviour can occur with dogs that are assessing the situation and potential trigger in the distance. By watching for tension, dilated pupils and face shapes you will be able to see how the trigger is being received by the dog.

Panting

Panting is the way that a dog cools off, because they only sweat a tiny amount through their paws, panting cools down their entire body in warm circumstances. It's also a sign that they are becoming worried, so if you see a dog that's not hot begin to pant – it's important to ask yourself why.

If you watch carefully you will be able to identify the onset of panting related to anxiety. The dog's closed mouth might open and close, sporadically panting for a short while before full panting begins. The intensity of panting is directly related to the dog's interpretation of the severity of the situation.

Panting escalates directly parallel to the level of stress, so the more stressed a dog gets, the more he will pant. Eventually if the stress reaction continues, the dog will pant with a wide gaping mouth, glassy eyes and he will probably also drool.

Other signals of mild to moderate stress may include:
- Cheek puffing
- Excess salivation
- Excessive shedding
- Freezing – little or no movement
- Low body posture, weight shifted back
- Stretching

- Sweaty paws
- Teeth chattering
- Tight brow
- Tightness around eyes
- Trembling/shaking
- Checking out his own genitals.
- Whale eye/ Half-moon eye
- Wrinkled muzzle. It's worth keeping an eye out for the signals described above and the signals listed. As the individuality of the dog you are observing will dictate his own unique combination of worry signs.

Shake Off

If the trigger goes away or the stressful experience ends in good time, the dog may shake off the stress he has experienced, much like he's shaking water off his coat. He may also shake off during a meeting or interaction with a person, dog or other trigger to lower his elevating stress response and keep himself calm.

Takeaway Points

- Many of us talk to our dogs but are not so competent at listening, we can learn to listen with our eyes.

- The more we know about early communication signals, the better we understand our dogs.

- When we adhere to early, subtle requests our dogs don't need to move to more extreme communication.

- Nobody wants to be ignored.

- We need to be sharp eyed to recognise early signs of discomfort.

- Early signs of stress are unconscious signals and conscious communications dependent on the situation.

- If early communication is ignored a dog is left no choice but to use more overt behaviours.

- If the trigger for stress is not removed when early signs are shown, the dog's stress level will escalate.

CHAPTER FOUR

Escalation into Stress

"Animals have come to mean so much in our lives. We live in a fragmented and disconnected culture. Politics are ugly, religion is struggling, technology is stressful, and the economy is unfortunate. What's one thing that we have in our lives that we can depend on? A dog or a cat loving us unconditionally, every day, very faithfully" —Jon Katz

If the smaller signals don't give the dog a break from his escalating anxiety, his posture may change, and the signs become more obvious. As stress escalates the dog's fight or flight reaction is triggered so his choices now are directly based on the environment and the way he has learned to cope with threats to his safety. It's important to remember that the dog's fight or flight reaction is not a choice, it's a push from the nervous system to act in some way. The only choice that the dog has is how to react in that moment and like every other choice, that is based on genetic inheritance and previous experience.

The most common option when a dog realises that encountering the trigger is unavoidable – unless he has learned it's impossible or pointless – will be to take flight. Getting out of the situation is the dog's way of avoiding injury through fighting or confrontation. Remember that by nature the canine species and his common wild ancestors most often seek to live in peace.

In the first instance if a dog can leave a scary or confrontational situation he will. If he can't he will either go directly to fight, or freeze and eventually when he has no other option he will fight.

Just like the communication process though, if the dog has learned that leaving isn't an option for him, the dog may go directly to freeze or bypass both and display willingness to fight. Even if the dog hasn't the strength or inclination to follow it through, he may just be trying to rid the environment of the trigger by a huge display of bravado. This often works, so like any choice that gets a favourable result – teaches the dog to repeat it with gusto next time he's in the situation.

Fear is an integral part of a dog's experience in the situation of escalating stress. As a strong and primal emotion, fear is powerful and can cause severe distress for a dog, particularly if he can't escape from the thing he is scared of. In addition, a dog can feel stressed for up to 72 hours after a stressful experience, leaving him more tense for up to three days.

The movements and signs explored below show both fear and stress.

Whilst canine fear is a big topic we don't need to have a vast scientific knowledge, in order to recognise fear in our dogs.

Hypervigilance

When a dog is scared he will show some common behaviours. The dog that senses a trigger nearby, usually through scent, will become hypervigilant and look around quickly, trying to locate the location of the trigger itself.

Distance has an important factor here, the closer a trigger is the more likely it will affect the dog. At a manageable distance for the dog, the dog will cope – it's only when the trigger gets too close for comfort that the dog's internal state will change.

When he locates the trigger and if it's too close for him to feel comfortable the dog's body begins to show us his internal state. Whilst I go through the subtler signs first here, it's important to remember that some may be skipped by the dog, based on his individuality.

Creeping

Creeping and moving slowly is a sign that a dog is starting to become tense. In the image below the dog's tail and hind quarters have dropped and he looks like he's trying to move carefully, perhaps away from his trigger. Note his tension around the lips and unmissable seal ears. The dog will avoid looking at or making eye contact with the trigger (if it's human or another animal).

Turning Away

Turning away from a trigger is associated with non-confrontation. A dog that is confident enough to fight or show aggression will not usually turn away because it puts the other animal in a place of strength. However, if a dog has no intention of confrontation they may consider turning away the ultimate gesture of peace, because it makes them vulnerable. The dog in this picture shows low body language/tail, tense lips and seal ears as he turns away in a gesture to avoid contact and/or confrontation.

Refusing Food

A common mistake we can make when attempting to help a dog cope with the world is take him into a stressful situation and try to feed him treats. The problem with this is that once the stress reaction has begun, the dog won't take the food. Stress switches the digestive and immune system to secondary importance, whilst preparing the dog for fight or flight. So, whilst food is an excellent tool for changing behaviour it is only effective if the dog's stress reaction has not yet begun.

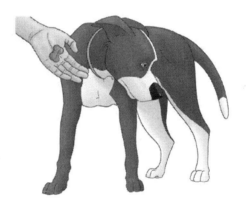

You may have heard the term "threshold" which simply means the point of no return. Try to imagine your dog's stress reaction like a snowball rolling down a hill and gathering snow and speed as it goes. At the beginning of the journey, you may be able to stop the newly formed snowball and even push it back up to the top of the hill, but the further and faster it goes the less likelihood you have of doing that. The stress reaction where your dog's signs are yawning, and licking may still be reversed, and the dog may still take food before you move him away from the trigger (which is vital to prevent escalation). Yet when your dog stops taking the treats that he loves, you can be sure that he's quite stressed.

Since my little Yorkie was attacked I use treats to measure her stress level when we are approached by an unknown, uncontrolled dog – of which there are way too many! If she takes them immediately after the dog has gone away she has recovered well from the invasion. If she refuses food she has taken it pretty badly because she loves food.

Appeasement

Rolling over is the ultimate statement of peaceful intention. It's an extremely vulnerable position for a worried dog and is used as an appeasement gesture. Appeasement behaviour is carried out to display peaceful intent and to avoid confrontation of any kind. It's the dog saying, do exactly what you like – I won't fight it.

There's a term in dog training called an alpha roll where poor quality trainers push a dog into this position to assert themselves. In their own misunderstanding, this type of trainer confuses the dog too – and such forceful, unkind physical manipulation also terrorises the poor animal. Exposure of the stomach in the dog and all canid species is predominantly a behaviour of choice, to communicate with peers.

The dog in this picture shows many signs of appeasement. His tail is tucked, belly exposed with lifted outer leg, ears out at the side of his head, his lips are pinched up and so is his brow. He certainly doesn't want to do battle and literally just wants to be friends.

The dog in this picture is also showing peaceful intention. The paw is lifted to show that's he's unsure, ears are out at the sides to show appeasement and face is tense. Sitting can be used to calm another animal and in this case, the dog is using his sit position as an extra signal that he means no harm.

Tucking In

A dog who tucks right under - like the picture below – is very worried. There are many signs of fear displayed by this dog. The head is dipped, whale eye is showing, A paw is lifted in this case as a sign of anxiety. The dog's rear is tucked under and his face is tense with tight lips and brow. A dog that is this worried, needs space from his trigger, without delay, even if that trigger is you.

At the point where a dog is scared his response will go one of two ways. He will try and hide within himself which is a tool of the dog with learned helplessness and particularly gentle animals. Or he will start to become defensive by flashing his teeth and working his way through a process into aggression.

Teeth Flash

As we know, the dog who shows his teeth is saying "I have weapons and am prepared to use them" He can do this from a place of fear or confidence and by looking at the rest of the dog, we will be able to tell which it is. Remember that confidence can be based on fear too – so the dog might still be scared but has learned to use aggression with competence when dealing with the trigger for his fear.

The dog in the picture below shows a fearful teeth flash. We are most likely going to see this position from a dog that is cornered and can't get away. Note how he's trying hard to turn away from us but also showing whale eye. He's watching to see what we do next. His ears are pulled back, telling us that the dog is scared. His face is tense, muzzle and brow tight and his pupils are dilated. Whilst he may appear offensive in his communication, a dog that shows all these signs is usually asking for his most basic right, personal space.

We might also see this expression when a dog is resource guarding, simply because he's asking for space specifically because he has a resource that he wants to keep.

Stalking

Stalking behaviour is generally an offensive act and we most often see a stalk from a dog that is interested in reducing space between himself and his trigger. The dog will usually have a hard stare, he may have dilated pupils, facial tension and a lowered stance. Stalking is a genetic behaviour originally used when hunting, it's also used in play. If an unknown dog stalks towards your own dog on a walk, with tension, slow movements and a hard stare, it's a good idea to get your dog to safety as quick as you can. Similarly, if your own dog does this he may have harmful intent, so should be fully under your control.

Antagonistic Pucker

Whilst the dog showing his teeth above is showing a defensive gesture, the pucker can also be antagonistic and instigative of a challenge. The dog in this picture is showing all his teeth in a gaping threat, his hackles are up, he is loaded with tension and is prepared to go to battle if he needs to.

The dog below also shows antagonistic behaviour. Note his tension and position along with a display of his teeth.

Bowing

When we begin to learn about dog body language one of the first things we usually learn is that a dog who bows is wanting to play. That's not always the case though because a bow is a position that can be attributed to almost any intention. The position itself is adopted by a dog because it enables them to move quickly in any direction. Dog may bow to play, he might bow and stretch in greeting, he could get in the position ready to pounce forward and attack (as above) or he might just be asking for space. Generally, a play bow is less intent on tension and the need to move forcefully and quickly, so the legs may be more splayed, and the dog appears somewhat goofy with a relaxed, soft face and body. Wolves have been known to bow when sizing up their prey.

Bowing and its many uses is another reason to look at every behaviour through the context that it is shown.

The final pictures in this module show a dog that is likely to bite if not removed from the situation. It's vitally important to pay attention to the earlier signals and respond with care, understanding and respect towards the dog to prevent any situation getting this far. If you are dealing with a dog that shows aggression regularly, it's important to first consult the veterinarian to rule out health and physiological problems then consult a scientific, qualified behaviourist to assess and help the dog.

Takeaway Points

- Stress and fear are intertwined in a dog's reaction and the body language that we see.
- Space is precious to a dog and the best option when a dog is scared is to give them space from the trigger for their stress.
- If you are the stress trigger and it's possible, move further from the dog and give the space back that he needs.
- Stress escalates like a snowball rolling down a hill and gathering speed and snow as it goes. You may be able to reverse it at the beginning by getting space between the dog and trigger but when it's fast and strong the process is unstoppable.
- A dog can feel stressed for up to 72 hours after a stressful experience.
- Most dogs won't choose aggression and confrontation to deal with a trigger, many will choose appeasement or calming body language. Aggression is often a last resort.
- Fear can be obvious or well-hidden behind defensive displays.
- A dog can be scared but extremely competent at using confrontation and even aggression to manage his fear.
- A bow means many things.
- Every behaviour and signal must be viewed in context to get an accurate idea of what the dog is experiencing and why.

CHAPTER FIVE

Confusion and Chatter

"While he has not, in my hearing, spoken the English language, he makes it perfectly plain that he understands it. And he uses his ears, tail, eyebrows, various rumbles and grunts, the slant of his great cold nose or a succession of heartrending sighs to get his meaning across" —Jean Little

When our dogs get confused they show us in no uncertainty exactly how they feel. Confusion is defined as uncertainty about what is happening, intended or required. When a dog becomes confused or uncertain he may become stressed, particularly if pushed too far despite his confusion – without being given any extra information.

If a dog becomes confused about what we expect, he is likely to feel conflicted. He knows that we want something but doesn't know what that something is. He wants to get it right but doesn't know how so that leads to a conflicted inner state triggering conflicted behaviours. Another term for the signals we see from a confused dog is displacement behaviour.

Here's an example of displacement behaviour in action and how it can be handled in two different ways, simply based on careful understanding, or lack of it.

Try to imagine that a dog is learning not to pull on the lead, for the first time in his life. Dogs are not born with collars and leads on so a slack lead is not natural to them. In fact, if someone put a collar and lead on you, out of the blue, you might just fight it too. I probably would. The teacher (which could be you or I with our dogs) in this case shows the dog what they expect by rewarding even the slackest lead and repeating that reward until the dog realises that not only does the teacher want a slack lead but also that they provide something nice in return.

If we move on too quickly the dog may become confused and show a sign of confusion – which is a communication to us, showing us to take a step or two back in the lesson to reaffirm our expectations. This is fair on the dog, because he's not a mind reader. The dog is happy, learns and the teacher understands him. Communication is perfect based on the our own knowledge of signs of canine confusion.

Imagine now that force based trainer is teaching a dog not to pull on the lead and doesn't make the lesson clear enough, so the dog becomes confused. Imagine also that the trainer doesn't understand about displacement behaviour and projects his own meaning onto the dog's confusion – for example he may assume the dog is being ignorant or dominant (heaven forbid). This trainer might become frustrated and blame the dog for his actions, which may include classic signs of confusion such as sniffing the ground or turning away.

In their frustration the trainer could try to force the dog to co-operate assuming the dog knows what they want. The dog will naturally get more confused and the stress reaction will begin. Unfortunately for the dog it's this point where force is introduced, there may be a check collar, general checking and the order to step back into line. This is a very sad situation for the dog because he doesn't know what's expected from him and now he's also being abused and getting stressed. All based on a dog trainer with a lack of suitable education.

We can avoid putting our dogs into uncomfortable situations and understand them better if we learn and look out for signs of confusion. Try to imagine conflicted behaviour as the dog showing us he is confused and that he might even be trying to change the subject.

Pacing

Pacing is a way to use the energy and avoid the point of confusion. Some dogs pace through being confused and some when they are starting to experience stress.

Scratching

Scratching himself frantically is a common way that a dog may decide to try and change the subject. To place the focus on something different is likely to be the dog's aim in this instance, he may be hoping that if he takes himself away for a short while, the situation will naturally resolve itself.

Sniffing

Sniffing the ground like someone has dropped the most wonderful scent onto it is a common displacement act. If you are trying to teach him something at the time, the dog may sniff the ground, or other things in the area and glance back at you occasionally, probably hoping that you change the subject too. This is a great opportunity to reassess your teaching approach and ask yourself if you are asking for more from the dog than he's able to understand or offer at that point.

Turning Away/Ignoring

This is one of the displacement signals that can get a dog into trouble if their handler or trainer doesn't understand canine confusion. The dog may turn away and just hope the problem that they can't solve simply goes away. Whilst this act may be misinterpreted as ignorance it's actually confusion and if it's treated as ignorance it will quickly become desperation.

Every dog will have his own signs of confusion. For example, one dog may sniff and yawn, whilst another may pant and scratch. This is because the experience of confusion and minor stress are very similar. So, my advice is that if you are trying to help your dog to understand you; whether that's via a lesson or something in your life together, watch out for any signs of confusion or signals of low level stress that we have covered in the book so far and if he's feeling conflicted your dog will most certainly tell you. When confusion isn't understood and if the person involved keeps pushing the dog, he will soon begin to experience the stress reaction of fight or flight.

Fooling Around

Fooling around is a lesser understood stress reaction. This is the response most likely to be observed in an environment where something is expected from the dog. For example, during teaching sessions the dog may try and change the subject by fetching a toy and throwing it in your general direction or playing with something that he's never really bothered with before. When he's confused on a walk or feeling worried a dog many jump up and grab the lead, he may nip hands and generally act silly and goofy. If this confusion escalates to stress on a walk, the dog could show height seeking behaviour, where he tries to jump up your body to cope with something in the environment or simply because he's not understanding your requests. Fooling around may also include humping behaviours, which can be carried out by dogs of either sex, for all sorts of reasons inclusive of anxiety and stress.

Any of these actions need true understanding. So, if your dog does these things, take a moment to assess why before you act then deal with the environment itself. Don't rush in and try to change the behaviour of the dog, because unless the environment changes, the dog's inner state will stay the same and so will his external symptoms.

Vocalisations

Whilst humans are vocal animals with the added bonus of a spoken language, dogs tend to communicate less through sound than they do through scent and body language.

Barking

Dogs bark to show happiness, fear, excitement, alarm, warning and even demand. Whilst we can understand each bark – to an extent - through its pitch, frequency and duration, other dogs probably learn much more from the sound of a bark than us, it is their language after all.

- A short sounding bark is often a signal of natural reflex to an emotion. Often short barks are given in fear or fright. A short bark may also be present if the dog is interrupted or distracted. It is possible to capture this behaviour unintentionally with reinforcement.

- Longer durations of barking suggest that the dog intends to use the sound on purpose. It may be to gain attention or even show warning to a perceived threat. Holding on to a certain bark is a way of saying 'I mean it'.

- Fast repetitive barking can indicate a sense of urgency. The quick-fire sound could happen during play or in response to a perceived threat, but the message is the same, 'now, now, now!'

- A single bark or barking with long intervals can suggest a lower excitement level. When a lower pitch is used, the dog may be attempting to appear large in a display of defence.

- Alarm barking is a high pitched and repetitive sound. It's used by a dog who is alarmed by something and telling us, or anyone else that there may be danger in the area. Also called spook barking, because it can occur when the dog gets a sudden fright, because he is spooked by a new or unexpected appearance of someone or something. This is usually accompanied by fright related body language of either a confident or fearful stance (depending on the dog).

- Demand barking or an attention seeking bark is high, excited and repetitive but it's also accompanied by excited body language and usually signs that the dog is enjoying himself.

- A happy and excited bark may be offered when somebody the dog knows enters the house or it is time to go for a walk.

- A mid pitch, repetitive bark often accompanied by excited body language and lots of movement. This bark will last as long as the initial excitement that caused it.

- Warning barks are often accompanied by other vocalisations such as growling. They will be short and low in pitch. A dog tends to become quieter and lower pitched if he is likely to be considering a bite.

Growling

Often growling is used in response to fear or threat but it is also used in play. Different dogs growl for different reasons and it's vital to always listen to the growl, assess why it's occurring and whether you need to make a change in the environment. Ultimately growling is precious communication and we should listen. Always remember that the growling dog is telling us something.

- Growling through fear produces a long low pitched sound. Its intention is to let others know that 'I am here' you should go away'. A dog may growl in fear at a sudden noise. If the growling does not stop the noise it may be followed up with an 'alarm' or 'spook' bark.

- Resource guarding can be used by a dog who has become

possessive over an item, food or a person. The dog may growl to warn others to keep away from the thing they consider important. Often this is a short, quiet sound but may become longer and louder if ignored. It is a way of communicating that he is willing to do what is necessary to keep what is his. This behaviour may include a short display of teeth when all else fails.

- Happy growling will sound very different to others. It may appear as a low pitch whine or 'grumble' depending on the dog. Often the dog will be rolling on his back, rubbing his face or enjoying a scratch.

- A play growl may appear as 'huffing' or whisper like, at first. Often the dog will growl only when an actual interaction occurs, either with another dog, human or toy. If excitement is added to the play, the growl may become louder and escalate into barking.

- The warning growl is often used in combination with a display of teeth. This growl will be long and loud, sounding very urgent. It is usually a final warning before aggression in the form of a bite.

A Variety of Vocalisation

A whimper or whine will be a high-pitched vocalisation. They are sounds intended to attract attention.

- A whining dog may be lonely, scared or frustrated.
- Often when a dog yawns in stress a high-pitched whine will accompany the action. A dog who is hurt will whimper, to

solicit care giving attention.

- Baying is a type of long drawn out howl/bark with a deeper pitch. This vocalisation is common in hound breeds who are trained to use the sound when following a scent. Beyond hound breeds, a dog may use this sound to challenge an unwanted intruder.

- Chuffing is the sound produced by a dog when they suddenly blow out a lot of air. The cheeks will puff out, then rapidly expel the air, creating the 'chuffing' sound. This vocalisation can be used as a greeting and may sound like a sneeze. A happy dog will chuff, sometimes several times in a row, as a kind of laughter or amusement.

- Howling in dogs lends its origins to the shared history with wolves. A typical wolf howl is sending one of two messages. A lone howl can be a call to an individual. A way of saying 'I'm over here, come and find me'.

  When a group howl together, it is often to appear larger in numbers and warn off anything that may have strayed into their territory. If a dog begins to howl at distant sounds, it may be this ancient behaviour acting out one of the two messages. A scared dog who is left home alone may howl to call his family back, creating safety and eliminating the fear.

- A sudden high pitched yelp from a dog is often caused by pain. The dog may have stepped on something sharp, hurt a muscle or been stepped on themselves. If the dog feels he has been hurt by another they may follow up with a frustrated snap of the teeth to say, 'get away from me'. This behaviour may also cause a dog to redirect their frustration, when they do not know who to blame for the cause of the pain.

The Importance of Body Language

Whilst I can't provide the sounds through this book I can describe them as accurately as possible. The most important thing to remember when listening to a dog is to also listen with your eyes. A growl with a tense body and face, hard stare and confident posture paints a different picture to a dog that is loose, playful, soft eyed and trying to instigate play with someone.

Always use all of your own senses to observe the dog and you will soon learn to understand not only how they are reacting to the environment but also what they are trying to tell you.

Takeaway Points

- When a dog is confused he will show displacement behaviour based in his own conflicted feelings.

- The dog may be conflicted because he wants to please us but doesn't know how to do it.

- Dogs can't read our minds (as far as we know).

- Displacement behaviour can be very specific signs such as sniffing or scratching.

- Sometimes dogs become stressed very quickly when they are confused, and their displacement signals are mixed up with stress signals.

- If a dog becomes confused we need to restructure our own communication or requests to make it clearer for him to understand.

- Vocalisations are always accompanied by body language and to fully understand them we must use our own senses to observe the dog.

- Vocalisations of all types are precious communication and should never be punished.

- We can work out what in the dog's environment is causing them to communicate through vocalisations and adapt that accordingly, which is the act of truly communicating with the dog, listening to their message and responding to it.

Quiz

This brings us to the end of the illustrated part of the book. From this point we will be moving onto exploring canine communication at a deeper level and looking at it through photographs of dogs and their communication signals. Before we do though, take a look at the images below and ask yourself how many of them you recognise immediately. Each of them are in the previous chapters so if you can't quite remember, it's worth going back to check.

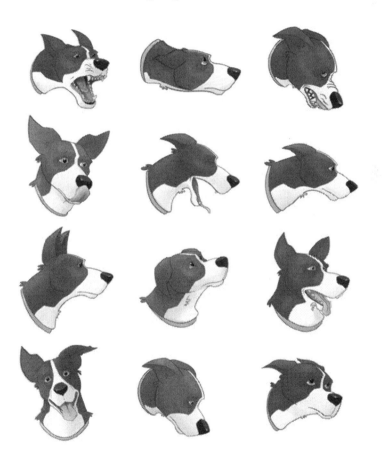

CHAPTER SIX

Meetings and Greetings

"The sense of smell in all dogs is their primary doorway to the world around them" —Robert Crais

Meeting and greeting between dogs is different to how people greet each other. This is often the reason we unintentionally intimidate

dogs, when we are trying to say hello to them. Intimidation through greeting is a bigger risk when we haven't learned to observe and understand canine communication.

There's a vague yet persistent historical theory on wolf packs based initially on observations of a captive group of wolves who were unrelated and pushed into an enclosed space. As the wolves were not living naturally, with their natural family, everything became very tense. The theory was created based on the tension in the group, that all wolves wanted to lead the pack. Now though, we know it was flawed science and we know much better.

If you have ever seen a natural, wild pack of wolves interact with each other, you are likely to have seen the family dynamics of the pack. Wolf packs are families, the mother and father run the pack and their cubs (both young and adult) are the pack members. Only the original parents breed. The parents of a wolf pack also guide the rest of their

family how to behave. The pack is a tribe, a history and a majestic group that is fundamentally also a close knit family of co-operators and relatives, just trying to live in peace.

Wolves are one of the most persecuted species and have been for many years. Even in nursery stories, the big bad wolf is cited as a sly, dangerous animal. They are accused of taking livestock and even untended human babies and children. Wolf families have been culled many times and like most animals that share the planet with the human animal, many types of wolf are endangered by our own growing species, planet destruction and resource control.

Compared to family dogs, wolf communication can appear overt. Nonetheless, even then it is based not on touch but body language and visual signals. Wolves do touch, just like our dogs do, but usually through play based on strong bonds or assertiveness. They can also touch through aggression which is extremely rare in a bonded wolf pack.

There's no disputing that dogs evolved from wolves, they share most of their DNA and strictly speaking are still the same species – because a dog and wolf can breed resulting in fertile offspring. We must understand though that dogs are not wolves and wolves are not dogs. One is a wild animal that has learned to fear humans based on much persecution over many generations. The other – the domestic dog – has evolved with a flawless bond to humans. The bond between dogs and people is so strong that even a dog who has been abused for many years will build an unflinching bond with the first human that introduces them to trust and kindness.

Seeing the two animals as different species with similarities is wise. One of the important similarities is the use of body language and visual signals as communication, as opposed to touch. Naturally dogs only touch when they are bonded, assertive or pushed into aggression. So, to go up and touch a dog without their consent is at total odds with the domestic dog's natural behaviour.

There is one other thing we must consider here, many domestic dogs don't get the chance to learn effective canine communication, because we interfere in their development. Social periods are bypassed without crucial learning, for many dogs which can leave them floundering in their attempts to communicate with their own species.

So, whilst we know that naturally dogs are perfect communicators, their behaviour often contradicts this because they haven't been provided with the chance to learn perfect communication, from patient and competent members of their own species. This is why dogs can appear obnoxious, ignorant and incapable around other dogs, for example jumping in their faces or bullying by not leaving the other dog alone when asked to.

As we know, domestic dogs are individuals. They will all have learned social skills from the moment they were born, they also have breed accents, which are genetic influence and dictate their finer communications to an extent. Witnessing two socially competent dogs greet and communicate with skill is a lovely experience.

A Perfect Greeting

A skilled greeting between two dogs has so many excellent signals of communication that I urge you to watch carefully at every chance you get, and you will see many of the signals we have already covered. The more you observe, the better and more skilled observer you will become.

When two socially competent dogs see each other at distance, they usually begin communicating immediately. If they want to say hello their body language will be relaxed and friendly. Their signals will be used to decrease the distance between them.

Distance decreasing signals invite the other party to come closer. They are used in many ways, some more useful than others.

The well-mannered dog that wants to greet will wag their tail and their facial expression will be relaxed and happy. Their body will stay relaxed and all this will tell the other party that they are interested in a greeting. The dog in this picture is totally relaxed and has a great big smile.

During the approach the dogs will read each other's signals. If one looks a little intense the other may briefly use a cut off signal such as glancing away and looking back. There's a lot happening at this point. The dogs are communicating their intention with skill and sharing information about each other. They might lick their lips or nose to show calm intent.

As they get within close proximity, a successful greeting will be characterised by two dogs that are either relaxed or suitably enthusiastic. If one is very enthusiastic and the other is offering cut off signals, which go ignored, this could result in the enthusiastic dog getting told off by the other one. Generally, though, a successful greeting is well-balanced.

Their eyes will be soft and so will their faces and bodies. Remember the tail position information, higher than neutral is an aroused dog and lower than neutral is a dog that feels unsure. As they greet, socially competent dogs will not directly approach the face of another dog but will seem to go by and check out the tail end first. A good greeting is curvy and avoids a direct stare or eye contact at all.

In this picture the puppy (Dobby 8 weeks) and adult dog (Douglas) are meeting for the first time, it's puppy's first day in his new home. The greeting is observed and managed. Look at the way the tiny puppy naturally turns his head slightly from the older dog. This is all new to him and the older dog is unsure but interested. See how his ears are pulled slightly forward, He also seems to be cheek puffing as he assesses the new, tiny clumsy stranger, which shows us that he's not entirely sure about this little invader yet.

Here they are again, and Dobby is making his way to the right end of his new friend. The puppy is doing everything right if he wants to be accepted by the still slightly tense older dog. Douglas is curving nicely, keeping his eyes on the source of his slight anxiety, yet not looking overly tense or using a hard stare. This is a nice greeting in a situation that's completely new to both dogs and the start of a beautiful friendship.

A dynamic between two dogs on greeting is established fairly quickly. Two playful dogs that want to play with each other will get down to delivering distance decreasing and play invitations almost immediately. They will wag, dance around each other for a moment or two, then one may offer a play bow and off they go. Sometimes though, even playful dogs won't play with a stranger immediately, yet will play with dogs they have greeted for a few minutes or a few times. Some will only play with a dog they are truly bonded with, and some dogs won't actually play at all. Some dogs just greet and move on. Neither wanting much more than a hello, just as we may say hi to someone in the supermarket but then feel terribly awkward if we keep bumping into them over and over again.

The two dogs in this picture are obviously happy in each other's company, both are interested in the other but look how they are positioned. Neither is interested in a face to face interaction, which is a perfect example of dogs not choosing eye contact even though they are interacting successfully.

Social capacity in dogs is similar to our own social skill and interest. Some of us go about our business in our minds, not paying much attention to other people and are happy in our own company. Whilst some people say hello to everyone they meet, chat about the weather and anything at all, for this person the subject doesn't matter it's the social interaction that's important. We also use cut off signals. For example, if we walk towards another person on a narrow pavement, with no way of avoiding the approach, we may glance away and pull out our phone to avoid even the smallest interaction with the stranger.

The way that our dogs handle the world and interactions is directly related to their personality. Personality is defined by genetic and environmental input – for example what they have learned about others and how they have learned to react to them. Dogs are introverts and extroverts, just as we are. If you're a quiet methodical person who is easily overwhelmed by others you will probably not appreciate being hugged by a stranger, just as a quiet, gentle dog won't want to be jumped on by an obnoxious member of their own species.

If we know our dogs well, we will already know which dogs approaching that they will appreciate, along with those we should really avoid. It becomes second nature to us to know which dogs will trigger certain behaviours from our own and cater our approach or ninja direction change accordingly.

In the same way, responsible dog walking dictates that we must consider others using the area and not allow our own dogs to initiate a greeting without the other person and their dog offering acknowledgement and most importantly consent!

On Lead Greetings

A dog who is on the lead may show different behaviour to one that is free to run away. Just as we see dogs barking and ranting behind gates and fences, we can see a similar barrier triggered behaviour from a dog on a lead, when they meet another dog. If we were to consider this with a dose of humour, the dog is brave from a distance. The truth is a little more sinister, the dog on a lead may be more defensive because they can't leave the situation. An inability to leave the direct physical proximity of a stranger, when you don't know that stranger's intentions, is enough to trigger anxiety in any of us. For our dogs, who have little true control over anything, it can cause the onset of a stress reaction.

Imagine you were stuck in a lift with someone and they were staring at you intently, how would you feel? Or perhaps you are at a dinner and have been seated next to a stranger that you don't like from the outset and they keep touching you and making you flinch. This is a similar situation we put our dogs into when we encourage and allow excessive or prolonged on lead greetings with other dogs that they don't know. They are tethered and potentially exposed to an irritating or threatening stranger in a situation from which they can't escape.

The dogs in this picture tell an excellent story. The dog on the left is interested but not threatening or overbearing. The dog in the right though is doing everything he can to avoid an interaction. Turning his face away in the way he docs here is a bold and definite cut-off signal that's screams "I don't want to interact at the moment, but I don't want any trouble either"

Every meeting between dogs will be a match or a mismatch of personalities and intentions. An immediate match is lovely to see, it's like when we meet someone we just click with, this often happens when one dog invites a second to play, at their first meeting and both dogs have a great time. Here's an excellent example of an invitation to play. The retriever on the left seems to have found himself greeting a keen youngster. He's trying different communication signals and the bow here has splayed front legs and is offering play as communication. The retriever also has slight facial tension, which is likely to be occurring because he's not quite matched with the puppy yet, so there's confusion.

The puppy in these pictures may be worried by the bigger dog, despite the bigger dog being interested and non-confrontational. The puppy on the right is lying down as a way of calming the situation and himself – whilst his new friend looks at him. The puppy's body language displays lack of confidence but a desire to interact. Look at his ears in the typical appeasement position.

In this picture the dog on the left, Rick, is trying to create a game with the Labrador on the right. The biggest sign of Ricks intention is the obvious play face. Add the face to the half play bow and side on position and Rick's asking his friend not only whether he wants to play, but which type of game he prefers. What a lovely, adaptive boy.

Sometimes it takes longer for a relationship to build between two dogs, then a match emerges as they align. This results in the building of a friendship between dogs which may or may not include play. Like any relationship that grows, dog friendship will be based on mutual choice and shared good experiences. This type of friendship is usually created by regular contact or sharing a home. Just like with people, first impressions count so if a new dog is being introduced to a home with existing dogs, creating a positive first meeting is crucial.

A good match on the lead is a possibility of course. We have all seen dogs that play whilst they are both on the lead, this is rarer than one or more of the on lead dogs finding an on lead greeting awkward or even stressful.

Negative and Danger Signs

A negative or dangerous mismatch on greeting is important to avoid for both dogs' sakes. On lead greetings should ideally not happen because of the added tension a lead involves. If they do happen they should be well-managed and observed carefully for all possible signs that either dog is struggling or considering confrontation. Even the necessary on lead greetings should be no longer than 2-3 seconds before the dogs are moved on, even if it's only for a few steps before they repeat the greeting. The body language signs that we covered earlier must all be considered when two dogs meet.

Danger signs include:

- A hard stare.
- Tension in the face.
- A furrowed brow.
- Tense lips.
- Ears pulled right forward or back on the dog's head, showing confidence or fear. Remember that floppy ears pinch at the side of the face when the dog wearing them is scared.
- A high tail and slow deliberate movements.

Here's an example of danger signs when two dogs are greeting on the lead. The Beagle on the right is taking an offensive stance, it could be due to well-hidden fear or a different personality trait. See how he is trying hard to make eye contact, has a hard stare and tense face, his tail is high and bristled and so is some of the hair on his back. The poor dog on the left looks like he would rather be anywhere else. His lips and ears are pulled back in tension, his posture is based in uncertainty and he looks vulnerable and worried. If you ever see or are party to a greeting that looks like this one, it's important to end it immediately and positively as tension is building quickly.

Submission and Dominance

Submission and dominance are terms that have been grossly misused and misinterpreted over the last few generations. Dominance and submission do exist in canine communication, but they are indicative of a point in time as opposed to a relationship or personality trait. Dominance may be shown when a dog is guarding a resource, making him dominant over that resource, whilst submission may be shown by another dog who just doesn't want the resource or is unwilling to fight for it.

Here's Lexi who is showing actual dominance over a resource. She loves that ball and will not allow anyone else to take it. Note the position of her ears, which only need to go out to the side of the head slightly to show guarding behaviour. The direct threat with her teeth, the hard stare and wrinkled muzzle. She means it.

Saying that a dog is a dominant dog is not particularly accurate. He may assume the dominant role in many situations, but the term describes the behaviour, not the dog. Similarly, a dog may default to appeasement behaviour regularly because the world makes them a bit anxious, yet they are not a submissive dog per se' they simply choose submissive behaviour as their way of coping in the world.

When we observe communication on greeting between two dogs we see how each of them are coping by their behaviour and stance. Each will not only greet how they have learned to greet others but during the meeting they will also be responsive to the other dog's communication and if socially competent, the dog will adapt his own accordingly.

The two dogs in the pictures below show an interesting greeting. The Greyhound is confident and has no worries about the other dog. The tan dog is taking a submissive approach – he may be trying to stay out of trouble.

Note how the Greyhound's stance is one of neutrality? He's nether aroused or worried, he's just there. The dog on the right is in a full on submissive role. She's trying very hard to be the Greyhound's friend almost to the point of grovelling.

Here she is again approaching the greyhound from an appeasement position. Her ears dropped right back, muzzle licking and staying in the peacekeeping position of sit. She's likely to be a much younger dog than the hound and just wants to make friends.

Appeasement Signals

Submission and appeasement are intertwined but show one important difference. Submission is about escaping the attention of the other dog whilst appeasement is about staying within the other dog's attention for long enough to announce peace. For example, in the case of Lexi above a wise dog would offer a sign of submission and get away from that stare as quickly as possible. They may show one appeasement signal and leave, submitting the ball to Lexi who has now become dominant over that resource. In the next pictures above, the tan dog is trying hard to be friends with general squirmy appeasement behaviour, she is torn between being unsure and wanting desperately to interact with someone of her own species.

Appeasing other dogs begins early, from the moment a dog starts clumsily playing in his litter or feeding from his mom he will learn that when he's too rough or nippy he will need to appease the other party as way of an apology. This is also the important time of learning about biting and how to self-inhibit their strength.

Bite inhibition is learned from mother and siblings then reinforced when the puppy moves to his new family. Puppies learn not to bite too hard through play and practice, then if they ever feel the need to bite, the natural inhibition gives them the ability to only use as much force as is necessary as opposed to all the jaw strength they have.

Appeasement behaviour can be used to attempt to create an affiliation, to show fear, to pacify and show peaceful intent. Dogs may also use appeasement behaviour because they literally can't escape and would rather take flight. It's really important that we understand this, so we are not assuming dogs are trying for affiliation but could easily be scared and trapped.

An appeasing dog is wriggly, lowered in posture, licking around the muzzle of another dog, they may wag their tail and entire hindquarters. Whilst many dogs may use this behaviour, our role is to assess carefully why they are doing it and adapt the environment to their needs. For example, an on lead greeting where one dog is showing appeasement acts may be because he's scared and can't escape, or an off lead game between a young and older dog may just be indicative of a puppy desperate to make friends. It's important to watch the other dog too if one is being particularly appeasing or pacifying, ask yourself why. Is the other dog enjoying the encounter or are they offering signals that they want to be left alone? If so, the encounter needs to be changed and managed too – for everyone's sake.

There's also a term labelled obnoxious submission where a dog is appeasing and submitting so much yet is in the face of the other animal, being pushy and overwhelming, that the behaviour is obnoxious. This type of act is often seen from dogs that haven't been taught manners by other dogs, or it may just be their personality. It's the equivalent of a person rushing up to us, getting in our personal space, patting our face and chattering wildly despite our obvious concern about their presence.

Here's a moment in time and a snap of appeasement gestures whilst

these two dogs interact. The little dog is going straight to the muzzle and his body is slightly tucked, he obviously wants to interact and isn't particularly worried – just stating his intentions. The bigger dog is wonderfully expressive, his ears are held high in a returned gesture of appeasement, his one paw is lifted, showing he may feel a little unsure, yet he is looking directly at his little appeasing assailant which tells us he has some level of confidence in the situation.

It's important to remember that each dog is an individual. With our own dogs – particularly when we can read their language – we become intuitive to what dogs they might like and which to avoid. We know when something won't go down well or when a dog sharing the park will be popular and a potential friend. Recognising individuality gives us an edge on understanding. The real skill is when we can recognise the individual signals of our own dogs and of every dog that we meet. This includes not only knowing how they are reacting to a trigger but how they are coping with the presence of each other, when two unknown individuals meet and greet.

Often other dog owners will reassure you their dog is fine - he just wants to play - but with your knowledge you may now observe situations where you know this isn't the case. You can therefore make informed decisions and move your dog on when you don't feel comfortable with another dog.

Takeaway Points

- When two dogs meet for the first time they will share a detailed communication.

- On lead greetings can cause unnecessary tension and should be avoided wherever possible.

- If both dogs are excellent communicators the meeting will either become a pleasant experience or end naturally as the dogs' part ways.

- Dogs always avoid eye contact with a new dog unless they are aiming for confrontation.

- If dogs communicate well and have the same intention for the meeting, we get a match.

- Common mismatches occur, just as we won't like all types of people our dogs won't automatically like all other dogs.

- A match may result in mutual play.

- A match may grow with a relationship or it may be instant.

- Dominance is a behaviour choice in a specific situation and not a personality.

- Submission and appeasement behaviours are similarly not personality traits, but behaviours that a dog may choose in a situation.

- Within a greeting, the behaviour of both dogs should be carefully observed. If one dog is not happy and not coping, we should end the greeting, or change the way it is being facilitated.

CHAPTER SEVEN
Distance Control

"No one appreciates the very special genius of your conversation as the dog does" —Christopher Morley

Dogs are natural negotiators, with us and each other. As individuals their negotiations skills will be unique to them and have been unarguably affected by human interference. Individuality dictates what dogs like and the things they would rather not be involved with.

Up to relatively recently dogs were considered clone like animals, with no uniqueness at all, an obviously flawed idea to anyone who has ever lived with them. Dogs are individuals with likes, dislikes, coping thresholds, preferences and slightly different needs.

Individuality of a dog will decide whether he is introverted or a natural extrovert and whether he enjoys meeting dogs in groups, for play and fun or whether he prefers a quiet meeting which he would still rather escape from. If a dog is introverted it doesn't mean that he's not social and never wants to interact, simply that he doesn't like crowds. Often being approached by an unknown, pushy, extrovert dog is far too much interaction for an introvert dog.

Some introvert dogs are happier with new people than they are with new dogs. Others are happier with dogs than people often based on which they have experienced their best and safest times with. Extraversion too can be affected by experiences. Holly, our Yorkie escapee from the puppy farm loves other dogs and started offering play the moment she moved in – at six years old – yet it has taken two years for her to happily play with our hands. Despite being a natural extrovert, Holly's experiences of people were so negative it took a whole third of her life again to realise we were safe to play with.

Interaction with other dogs and people is based on personality and learned traits, for every dog. Social competence and a desire to interact between two matched dogs dictates a good interaction. Even dogs that are not a match for play or friendship; but are socially competent, will have a successful interaction based on mutual respect.

Distance Awareness

Distance awareness is a vitally important area of social competence between dogs and between us and dogs when we communicate with them. Try to imagine that every dog has three invisible rings around them. The rings signify the dog's safe and comfortable distances from certain things. They literally tell us when the dog goes from feeling safe to feeling unsafe.

Social Distance

Social distance is the dog's personal space with his peers, human or animal. It's individual to the dog and can be defined by how willing a dog is to cuddle and snuggle up with his people and other animals in the home. It's possible for a dog to have a smaller social distance with people than dogs or the other way around, depending on their individuality. In this picture Buckley and Dixie are bonded and their social distance is very close indeed.

There's a slight difference in the comfortable social distance of these two. The dog in front is using a natural yawn to calm himself and calm the other dog because of their proximity and possibly because she's also looking at him. Note his paw lift too which is a sign of feeling unsure or vulnerable along with the slight splay of his back legs.

Flight Distance

As we already know flight is part of the stress reaction. The term flight distance is linked to how close something can get to an animal before that animal takes flight. When a dog is scared and has total freedom to run, with no prevention or prior learning that they are trapped they will run when something scary penetrates their flight distance.

Any learning or prevention of the ability to flee will give the dog no other option than to fight. So, the dog may feel he has to use an aggressive display or response, simply because he can't escape. If this occurs a few times, the dog will learn that flight isn't usually an option so will stop trying to avoid conflict and try to scare the trigger away instead.

Critical Distance

The critical distance is where the dog feels that aggression is his only option, so he literally thinks he has to fight for his life. This is a terrible experience for a dog and may result in an explosive attack.

A breach of both flight and critical distance may read here like they don't happen often but unfortunately they happen more often than they should, but their severity and effect on the dog is not recognised. The dog that we consider reactive is behaving that way because his flight distance has been breached. When we walk a worried dog on the lead and a loose dog approaches and gets in our space, our on lead dog is suffering with breach of his flight distance and his critical distance which causes physical stress that can last up to 72 hours.

This is why it's vital that we keep this in mind for all dogs in all areas. If you have a friendly dog then teach him to come when called and don't assume that all dogs want to interact, don't let your dog invade the space of others. If your dog does react, build his resilience to help him get through the world, teach him that there are choices and don't take him into places that he can't cope with until you are sure he is ready.

There are many signs and signals that dogs display to attempt to control their personal space. Often they go unrecognised. Two socially competent dogs will read each other's space maintaining signals perfectly. If we learn and observe, we too can read and adapt our own behaviour and interaction to the dog's communication.

Increasing Distance

A dog that is trying to make his personal space bigger by telling another individual to retreat or not continue their approach will use distance increasing signals. A dog that has learned to be reactive will use a whole jumble of these signals and lots of noise, literally warning the other party to stay away, or else there will be trouble. Ironically though these dogs rarely want any trouble; which is exactly why they are so loud in the first place, they just want to maintain their space and it's how they have learned to do that.

Controlling the distance via a set of communications is particularly important for a dog who is fearful, but all dogs should have the choice of whether they interact or not. Everyone is entitled to personal space.

Dogs will eventually show antagonistic behaviour as a communication aiming to send another individual away. It may begin with cut off signals, at a distance, telling the other party they are not interested in an approach. This dog is showing a nose lick as a cut-off signal, asking the photographer to give them space. A lot of dogs are uneasy when a camera comes out as it's an odd position for them and one which can appear as a direct stare. Note her ears out at the sides, whilst she licks she also uses her ear position as an appeasement gesture.

A dog will move their head in a certain way when trying to maintain their space, they may turn or dip their head lower than their body. The dog in this picture is dipping their head, licking, squinting and pulling his ears right back. He is also trying to appear smaller than he is in a gesture of appeasement.

The same dog here shows more tension in a different position. The lips are pulled right back in facial tension, this is a very worried dog that desperately needs some space.

They could possibly yawn or lick their lips like Lucy the Poodle in these pictures, which tells us she's not entirely happy with the proximity of the child.

Here's another dog that is being touched but really doesn't want to be. Look at the head turn, squinty eyes, ears pulled back and tension around the dog's face. It all shows us that the touch is unsolicited and not welcome.

From a distance an unwilling dog could perform a definite, tense stare and high paw lift that tells the other party in no uncertain terms not to approach.

If the other party doesn't adhere to those polite requests the dog may show warning signs.

In this picture the dog is guarding something she wants to keep. She is asking for space with her ears, tension and a hard stare, note her dilated pupils. At this distance she will not progress to a more overt warning but if her obvious body language is not adhered to and the other party continues to approach, she is likely to escalate into an aggressive response. The side ears are a common sign of resource guarding. Dogs can show other, socially competent dogs and people not to approach a resource, or approach them at all just by a slightly different ear position. This picture shows a wonderfully competent communication through eyes and ears, telling the other party not to come any closer.

Here's another image of a dog who is showing similar signs. This dog also shows a head dip. The hard stare is present, and we would be extremely unwise to approach her as she's telling us in no uncertain terms to respect her personal space. Note how she also has her ears to the side but because of her physiology they look different.

Whilst the communications in the pictures above should be enough to halt an approach, they often aren't because the approaching party can't read them properly, or misunderstands what the dog is saying.

If a dog experiences fear on the approach of someone else their ears are likely to be pulled right back, maybe even to seal ear expression, they may squint too and try to look smaller. However, if the approach

continues they may switch from peacekeeping to defence.

This dog is scared, note how her ears are pulled back and face is tense. The most telling part of this picture though is her hunched up body.

She's worried and trying to be smaller.

A dog that shows defensive distance increasing acts may show their teeth, growl, bark or even snap into the air towards the other party. All of these acts should make things clear to anyone observing that it's time to back off. Unfortunately, if the advancing individual isn't listening or doesn't understand they may continue to approach. Children, some adults and many poorly socialised dogs will advance towards a dog giving off a clear warning, and this is why dogs often end up biting.

Some dogs will muzzle punch to physically tell the other party to go away. This behaviour is carried out with a closed (or slightly open) mouth and the punch can happen once or repeatedly. The dog will have a tense face, hard eyes and the punching will usually be quite powerful.

 The dog in this picture is displaying an antagonistic pucker, note the dilated pupils showing us that his nervous system is already preparing for fight or flight. The dog's muzzle is puckered, ears pulled back and he's showing a whale eye along with a hard stare.

The antagonistic pucker is displayed in lots of different circumstances and for many reasons. The typical facial position is like the one above and if it's being used as a threat or prelude to aggression the dog is extremely tense with a hard eye and definite stare. This dog will posture tense and high he may hackle with a high bristling tail showing confidence.

Hackling for dogs is similar to goose bumps for people. They can occur through nerves or fear but of course if a dog has learned to (or is forced to) deal with their fear through aggression the hackles will also show as part of an aggressive communication.

This facial position can also be used by a very scared dog who has tried everything to be left alone and the antagonistic pucker may be their last attempt to increase distance before they bite. For this dog the body language will be very different. They may be trying to look smaller, turning away slightly and their tail could be tucked underneath them. This dog may never have considered biting but because the scary thing is advancing and not listening to them, they may believe they have to bite in order to survive.

Decreasing Distance

Just as dogs use signs to increase the distance and cut off any chance of interaction they also show clear signs that they are happy for the distance between them and the other party to decrease. This allows nice relaxed greetings or play between dogs and physical affection to be shared between dogs and people. This type of communication tells the other party they can feel safe to approach without worry or anxiety. It can lead to rewarding interactions and play.

Communication signals show a lot of behaviours used in different ways so it's always important to read the dog and the environment carefully. All dogs have slightly different signs but remember to look for the tense body, high tail and hard stare – if these occur the dog is

likely to be feeling tense. Yet if the dog is loose, wagging and interested when he shows some similar shapes, he is probably keen to interact. Milo here looks happy and friendly, relaxed and has a lovely big smile.

The picture below is interesting because the smaller dog is approaching the larger dog's muzzle as a distance decreasing signal whilst the bigger dog is the object of his communication. There's also a little dog between them showing a clear paw lift, head dip and nose lick an as distance increasing gestures.

Dogs do carry out splitting behaviours which serve to break any tension between two other dogs, or even a dog and person/other animal. There's wonderfully telling communication here. Despite the dog that is in the middle looking like they would rather be anywhere else in the world, they are trying their best to keep the peace.

A play bow is another distance decreasing gesture. The willingness to interact and play will be defined by a play face, soft eyes and general goofy behaviour. It's an invitation to have some fun.

Here's another bow, this time from a different breed, Rory is stretching and bowing at the same time, soliciting interaction as a distance decreasing act. The exact way a dog uses the positions may look different to the way they look on other dogs. Rory's bow looks long, stretched out and relaxed, probably because he's relaxed and happy in his home. His mouth and facial features are relaxed, he even looks like he's smiling, and his tail is high and confident which goes with an overall relaxed bow aimed at someone he loves.

You might see this type of position from your own dog on greeting. It's a communication of happy greeting, and a distance decreasing bow that also shows how bonded they are to you. It's quite wonderful really. Other distance decreasing acts include a wagging tail and body, little  bops with the muzzle and sometimes a submissive grin delivered in the style of the one below. The dog may grin when rolled over, when approaching another party or even when they play bow.

Takeaway Points

- Start observing dogs based on how they might be feeling and assess how their personal space is being respected.

- Assess your own dog's comfortable social distance and how they work to maintain it.

- Flight distance is an ancient evolved part of fight and flight response which occurs in the dog's nervous system.

- Many dogs have learned that flight is not a viable option for them, so they show defensive acts (fight)

- Dogs will show distance control acts which serve to send another party away or invite them to come closer.

- The other party will respond with respect if they fully understand the distance control communication signals.

- If the other party cannot understand and continues to approach this causes stress and conflict.

- It's up to all of us to respect every dog's personal space whether we live with them or meet them elsewhere.

- We must prevent our own dogs approaching a dog we meet unless the other dog and their human has given a clear invitation and permission.

- Everyone is entitled to personal space.

CHAPTER EIGHT
Play

"When we adopt a dog or any pet, we know it is going to end with us having to say goodbye, but we still do it. And we do it for a very good reason: They bring so much joy and optimism and happiness. They attack every moment of every day with that attitude" —W. Bruce Cameron

Play is a Universal language for dogs. It's the epitome of their ability to live in the moment and have fun just for the sake of it, which is something us humans try to learn to do constantly, most recently through mindfulness but seem to find difficult.

The reasons for canine play has recently been explored by scientist Marc Bekoff, who summarises that dogs play just for the sake of it in many cases, which is wonderful. The basis of play communication is two or more dogs on neutral ground, with one intention, to have fun. Dogs that play well know that if they become too overt, scary or rough the game will end. Any kind of intimidation during play is unacceptable and self-inhibition of physical intent is an important part of play co-operation.

There are many styles of play and all dogs have their preferences. The chosen play depends on breed, learning and individuality but the fundamental evolved behaviours associated with play have a deep set genetic basis. Play behaviours match the dog's hunting skill of his pre-domestication and when a dog plays we can still see the hunter predator in there somewhere, though with play it's all about equality and maintenance of the game.

The Sequence

Predators that hunt and catch other animals for food and to feed their families do so as part of a sequence. The ancestors of the domestic dog, plus his wild canid cousins still practice this sequence for survival. Whilst our dogs don't need to hunt now, the DNA of his ancestors are still within him, mostly diluted thankfully but the dog still gets to act out the sequence through play. It's these behaviours which we will explore in more detail throughout this chapter.

A successful hunt for the wild cousins of our domestic dogs includes stalking, chasing, catching killing and eating their prey. The process is finely tuned, and the play habits of our dogs began as part of this innate sequence many generations ago.

Play body language is wild and wonderful. If we were to walk into a situation where two overt dogs were playing loudly we could be forgiven for thinking they may be working towards a fight. There is an excellent, subtle communication through play though that includes keeping the game even, not pushing the play partner too far and self-inhibition to maintain the game.

Whilst we discuss only the play aspects of the sequence here it's vitally important to be aware that many of these behaviours are also used for other communication types, for example the intention of aggression or to show fear. It's really important to watch the entire dog and not to make assumptions on one or two behaviours.

Play body language will be punctuated by meta signals that are delivered to keep the peace and maintain the game. If a playing pair don't maintain a relationship as equals, the game will end.

Types of Play

Play happens in many different ways from the sheer enjoyment of running in circles to throwing a toy around. Dogs play on their own, with us and with each other.

Movement based play is sometimes called locomotor play. It's defined by a dog playing by moving his body quickly and having fun along the way. Whilst we may dance, dogs do something similar with their locomotor games. The term 'zoomies" is a well-known type of locomotor play.

Here's an example of a happy dog, mid zoomies with a play face and play bow. She's loving the movement just for the sake of it and is asking for her human to join in. What a compliment!

Here's another example of locomotor play with my own dog Vinny. He's running in the snow with glee and his crazy play face shows us how much he's enjoying it. Vinny is showing all his teeth here which in different circumstances would have an entirely different meaning. In this scenario though, my little dog is grinning all over his face.

Chasing each other is a type of movement based play. The chase is an important part of the prey sequence too but generally with well-balanced play, it's just a game. It's really important to monitor chase games initially. Some dogs are bred to chase and catch smaller animals, sighthounds in particular have a long genetic history of chasing prey so no risks should be taken and it's particularly unwise to allow sighthounds to chase unknown smaller dogs. Be breed savvy and observe carefully all times.

The two dogs in this picture are combining locomotor play and object play. The dog in front has the prize whilst the second one is giving chase, maybe just for the prize or perhaps because he is simply enjoying the chase.

Object Play

Object play is prize based. It may once have been prey based but it's now usually toys and other objects. There are many types of object play, from the puppy throwing a pine cone around at the park to a pair of dogs having a noisy game of tug with a ragger.

Here's an amazing picture of solo object play and complete enjoyment of the game. We can facilitate object play for dogs by providing them with toys that they like and even associating those toys with natural tasks for example the snow in this picture makes object play more interesting for the dog and is naturally enriching his ball play experience.

Solo object play is pretty common. When dogs live in groups they often carry out group object play too. Some love to share a toy and play a game of negotiation with it. Whilst some dogs don't like to share at all, so would never play tug with anyone – instead keeping the object to themselves and warning others to stay away. Every dog is capable of mutual object play and sharing for the sake of a game, if they learn it early enough or get the lesson from a socially competent dog.

These three are having a grand time with one toy between them. There's no hostility obvious in any of their immediate positions and the dog on the left, although staring a little, seems to be mid play face.

When two or more dogs are playing with an object and one of them decides that want it most, it's a really interesting transformation to watch. The game changes and then ends because one dog tenses up, he may make more noise and his face becomes a hard stare. The dog who wants the toy or object literally does the canine equivalent of squaring up, his body gets tense and posture heightens. The other dog then, unless he decides the object is worth fighting for, will hand it over and go and find something else to do. The game is over.

As with all play, dogs will self-inhibit during object play to maintain the game. That's why we see dogs who are a mismatch of size and strength playing with an object with equality. The game is more important than the object for these dogs and that's communicated between them perfectly.

The puppy in this picture is getting an important lesson on playing tug, whilst the adult dog self-inhibits both to maintain the play and teach the puppy about equality in play.

Using Tug for Low Confidence Dogs.

If you play tug with your own dog it's important that you too maintain that equality in the game. Playing tug with a ragger or other toy is a great way to build the confidence of a dog who lacks self-belief. They might not initially put much effort into pulling on the toy because they have low self-esteem but if you let them win a lot in the beginning by releasing the toy into their possession, your dog will grow in confidence – just as we all do when we succeed at something. Let the toy go and make a big deal that he won it and your dog may even start to parade his toy around with the glee of a champion. After just a few sessions of building up your dog by letting him win, you will see the courage of his conviction in this game and that confidence will spill over into other areas of his life. This happy dog is showing a typical *lap of victory* behaviour because he's won the prize and feels great about it.

Important note

Whilst letting your dog win to build his confidence is a great idea for dogs that lack self-belief, it's not a practice that's suitable for all animals. Dogs that are susceptible to resource guarding for example may find tug games stressful and for these dogs it's a good idea to replace tugging with swapping to show no-one wants their stuff. The lesser importance placed on a potential resource, the less likely a dog is to guard it.

Stalking

Some dogs stalk a lot whilst others rarely do it at all. Stalking is predatory behaviour and during equal play is harmless and just another part of the game. Dogs may stalk up to a toy and pounce on it.

They may stalk up to familiar dogs and transform into a play bow or game, or part way through an existing game, during a natural pause a dog may stalk to restart the play.

The border collie is a stalker by nature based on his role as a herder of sheep. In this picture the dog has gone into a typical initial stalk position whilst he assesses the thing that has caught his eye. Border Collies are extremely visual dogs and genetically have the visual ability to notice even the smallest movement in the environment because they have been bred that way.

When dogs that are playing stalk a dog that they are playing with, the actual stalking motion may only be momentary. It can start and develop into something else – such as a pounce – so quickly that we may only see it if we filmed the game and slowed down the recording. This picture shows a perfect stalk with a game in mind.

During a hunt a dog's ancestors would stalk, perhaps bow then pounce or grab at their prey with their teeth. We see this all the time with dogs that play together. There is one big difference though, play is about negotiation and role reversal - the aim is to maintain the game. So, a well matched pair of dogs will take turns to be predator and prey, they self-inhibit and use distance control, appeasement and perfect communication when playing.

Here's a lovely example of a pounce during play.

Play based in catching the opponent/prey must be respectful and self-inhibited or the other dog will get hurt. This stage of play depends on how willing the individual dogs are to play roughly. Some dogs really love a big, noisy rough game whilst others would find this intimidating. Just like the success of a meeting depends on well-matched dogs, so does a well-enjoyed game.

For example, one of my dogs, Chips, is extremely vocal. He might poke with a paw and do a lot of bowing and growling. If the other dog understands him they join in a noisy game. If the other dog is not used to that noise, he can be extremely intimidating; and the other dog would rather leave than have anything more to do with him.

Many dogs will chase and go no further with the game. Some may chase then go through the ritual of the original kill, with mutual respect. They might pounce, bite legs or muzzle wrestle as part of the game.

Play biting is a common part of play, but it's always inhibited; and both dogs must give permission to play that way. A dog might bite the neck, throat or legs of another dog which has evolved from the hunt but is now just a game for our dogs.

The dogs below are playing yet it could all look pretty scary if you didn't know that. Their behaviour is complete co-operation. Skye underneath is taking the losers role in a feigned fight and role reversal is likely to soon occur.

Here's another image which shows similar use of the mouth during play. Both dogs are happy and the smaller one on our left has an excited play face. It may be based on a kill bite from long ago but it's now fun for the sake of it, which is brilliant.

Dogs must practice excellent bite inhibition during play. They only need to hurt a play partner once or twice to lose their rights to play with them at all. No-one wants to be hurt in a game and dogs will avoid a strong nipper and their painful play bites. If one bites too hard, the second dog may bite hard back, resulting in a squabble, then an end to the game, followed by an unwillingness to play again.

These two dogs are muzzle fencing, both are self-inhibiting. The dog on our left has his paw lifted which could be his affiliation sign, telling the other dog that this is all in good fun.

These two dogs are mid game, the paw lift in this instance is an affiliation signal, dogs often jab another with a front paw when they are trying to initiate play. The dog on the left may be a little less at ease in the game than the other one based on his leaning a little back, ear position and a little whale eye, or it may just be a snapshot on what seems to be a game based on equality.

Dogs are amazing negotiators. If their socialisation period has been affected by lack of positive development, their negotiation skills may be a little lacking. However, as a species they naturally avoid conflict and work together with others, often to achieve a specific aim.

Wolves are better negotiators with each other if they are given a task, their natural reliance on their family group makes the wolf an excellent team player with his own species. We, as the domestic dog's peer group now, are often the object of their negotiation skills for problem solving. This is particularly true in one dog households. Dogs often look to us to help with problem solving. The good news about this is that we can set problems and help the dog to solve them in a way that's greatly enriching to our dogs and our bond. It's also important to set your dog problems that they are capable of solving on their own, then encourage them in a way that builds their confidence and self-worth.

Puppy Licence

Negotiation begins early with puppy licence. Just like human children manage to push the boundaries of what they can get away with because they are learning, so do puppies. Puppy licence allows puppies to do much more with other dogs, who are patient and allow learning behaviour because the puppy needs it. A socially competent and confident older dog will allow a puppy to exercise his licence whilst also teaching the youngster when he has gone too far. The adult dog in the picture below looks a bit fed up of the puppy who is casually and competently exercising the licence of his youth.

Predatory Drift

Predatory drift is the act of play becoming serious. Predatory based play such as fighting, or chase can, very occasionally become serious and result in an attack. Predatory aggression is where the lines are blurred between prey and other animals in the moment for the dogs involved. It's vitally important to watch play carefully for any signs that things may be getting out of hand. Be especially careful about small and large dogs that are not bonded, playing together. Be aware also that squeaky dogs may trigger a natural predator response from some dogs. This is an extremely rare behaviour in the domestic dog but with knowledge and excellent observation you can watch for the warning signs. If things look tense between playing dogs, stop the game and allow them to cool down.

Takeaway Points

- Dogs are excellent negotiators.
- Good and positive social learning will hone the negotiation skills of any dog.
- Poor or lack of social learning affects communication skills and often the knowledge and natural ability to negotiate.
- Play is a game of equals.
- A lot of play behaviour is based on ancient hunting rituals such as stalk, chase, pounce and kill.
- Play fighting is also an ancient ritual.
- The aim of dogs that play together is simply to maintain the game.
- During play an equality of role reversal is important to keep the game going.
- Puppy licence ensures that puppies can push the boundaries of interaction whilst they are learning.
- Social competence is created by positive social learning.
- Whilst it's unusual play can become serious and result in aggression from one of more of the dogs involved.

CHAPTER NINE
Conflict

"Dogs do speak, but only to those who know how to listen"
—Orhan Pamuk

During this module we are going to look at aggressive behaviour and conflict. The aim of this part of the book is to help you to recognise and avoid conflict at its earliest point. It's really important that if your dog is showing aggression of any type, you first go to the veterinarian to check for pain and physiological changes then get help to help your dog. It's always a good idea to get help, even if you are highly educated in dog behaviour. Two observations and assessments on one behaviour are much better than one, especially if one of them is objective.

Aggression

The first thing to learn about aggression is that it's a totally natural behaviour in some circumstances. For example; self-preservation is a trigger for an aggressive response for all of us. If we really feel we are in danger and have no other choice, we will aggress, it's an evolved response and one that seems to happen all on its own.

That said, regular conflict and aggression are really not a well-balanced dog's style. To stay safe dogs won't fight. They negotiate to stay in one piece. Aggression is real though and can occur for a number of reasons. If we know or live with a dog that show's aggression our role in the first instance is to learn why. It's important that no risks are taken towards a dog that may show aggressive tendencies.

One of the old fashioned dog training methods was to trigger aggression in order to punish the dog for the behaviour. We still see this in some circles and not only is it unfair and cruel to the dog, but it's also pointless because every behaviour practiced will get stronger.

An aggressive response needs to be carefully analysed whilst the dog shows the earliest symptoms that his behaviour is heading that way, then neutralised way before it develops further. It is a job for a specialist really, for a couple of reasons. It can be really hard to take an objective view of our own dog's responses and behaviour because we are emotionally attached, a second pair of eyes is always good help particularly if they have carefully studied aggressive responses in dogs. If you add an objective and subjective view together, we are most likely to fully understand our dogs at the time they most need our help.

Dogs can be aggressive to other dogs, or to people and other animals. It really depends on their individuality. It can also begin inside the dog as part of physiological change, or an aggressive response to something in the external environment.

Internally Triggered Aggression

- Idiopathic aggression is rare but describes an aggressive behaviour for no apparent reason. The term idiopathic simply means no explanation. Many clients consider their dogs as showing this type of aggression yet with professional exploration there is often another reason.

- Medication based aggression, some medications can change a dog's behaviour from the inside, usually as a side effect.

- Pain and illness related aggression is based on a dog that is in pain and stressed. This can take the form of a panic bite when physically trapped or fearful of being hurt.

- Physiological and biological aggression is caused by sickness or chemical changes within the body. Thyroid disease is linked to this type of aggression along with canine cognitive dysfunction and other biological brain changes.

Externally Triggered Aggression

- Alliance aggression is shown when a dog is in the company of someone they have an alliance with, this can be the dog's primary caregiver or other dogs with which they have an alliance. This can also take the form of group related aggression, dogs that only show the behaviour when in a group of other dogs.

- Barrier aggression stems from feeling helpless to escape for example on the lead. Another type of barrier is a fence or gate where friendly dogs will fight through the barrier, where normally they wouldn't. This is termed barrier frustration.

- Fear aggression as already discussed can be part of flight or fight. If the dog is unable to leave the situation or is cornered eventually they will show an aggressive response. The exception to this is if the dog is suffering with learned helplessness in which case they will go into emotional shutdown and freeze to wait out the threat. Fear aggression is also known as proximity sensitivity.

- Maternal aggression is a mother protecting her puppies if she believes they are in danger.

- Redirection is aggression that moves away from the dog's primary focus and into his immediate area. This is one of the reasons a handler will be bitten if they try to break up a dog fight with their hands or feet. They are not the target of the aggression, but they are the closest thing to the dog's mouth. Redirected aggression can also occur if a dog is on leash behaving aggressively and frustrated and then turns around to bite the handler.

- Resource guarding is a type of competitive aggression where the dog is competing for anything that he sees as a valuable resource. This can be a vast range of things, from getting into an area first, attention of the caregiver or food and toy resources.

- Response to punishment. A dog that is punished by their

handler may show an aggressive response, this is particularly so if the dog has no means to escape the punishment. This is a form of fear and pain aggression elicited via the rough handling of the dog and can be misinterpreted as a further challenge by the human who then escalates the punishment.

- Territorial aggression is the guarding of territory or property. It is a type of resource guarding and can be relevant to everything the dog sees as his property or the property of his human caregiver.

We must consider each domestic dog as an individual animal. Not only a product of their genes, but also their mother's life during gestation, what they learned after birth and in their lives so far. That said, we can assume that some domestic dog breeds will have benefited from genetic traits that included aggression, even if it was only to maintain their relationship with their human handlers. Terriers for instance, that work in the field and dogs that were (and sadly still are) bred for fighting. In addition, even domestic dogs fear loss of resources, and so aggression is a trait that they may find helpful in guarding those resources.

Finally, it's an aspect of communication, most of which is useful in meeting their needs and getting their point across.

Aggression that begins in illness, physiological changes or pain needs to be treated by the veterinarian without exception. Often when the pain or problem is taken under veterinary care and control the dog will start to recover behaviourally too. An example of physiological aggression is the older dog who has begun to feel pain in his joints. Without treatment and lifestyle changes this dog will become unhappy and likely defensive, displaying signs that he doesn't want to be touched in case it hurts. He might start to guard his personal space. Supplements and medication may slow down deterioration and manage the pain, meaning that the dog feels better – although we should still be respectful of his personal space.

Externally triggered aggression is something we have a little more control over. Simply because we can control the environment at the same time we consider the dog's state of conflict. It's actually extremely rare to live with a dog intent on conflict; particularly if we fully understand the dog and his motivations, plus respect his natural rights.

Communication of Conflict

An aggressive response is based on internal conflict. For example, the dog is eating and wants to be left in peace, but we insist on fiddling with him, that dog may believe he needs to protect his food. Or if the dog has something they consider of high importance and we take it away they may feel the need to show through a lip lift or growl that they want to keep their things.

We seem to have evolved extremely high expectations of dogs instead of respecting their rights as individuals. We want them to give up everything they like if we decide we want it, not show they are uncomfortable in situations and be exceptional with children messing with them like they are toys. We expect dogs to be beautifully social despite our own efforts at helping them develop socially being patchy or uninformed. A growl in many instances is considered a sinful act when really it's beautiful, perfect communication.

If you live with a dog how much space does your dog get and what are the expectations of him? Is he expected to be perfect, without fail and roll over to your every whim? Or do you treat him like the unique, individual animal that he is? Do you give him space, let him have his own things without you threatening to take them away? Does your dog eat in peace and do you not only communicate with him but also listen to and respect his requests?

Only in a neutral relationship with no judgement of your dog and all respect of his communication attempts will you reach the point where you live as unique, individual equals sharing a space with true, wonderful and balanced understanding.

The Build Up

Conflict becomes aggression if it's not resolved. Conflict can be something simple like being approached whilst chewing a particularly tasty treat or being approached on a walk after sending lots of distance increasing signals then being ignored.

Submission

No-one likes conflict but often it is out of the dog's control, he would usually rather retreat than aggress. The only exception is the dog that has learned over time that retreat is not possible. The picture shows a dog that is intimidated and worried by a cat. This dog has likely learned that the cat is spikey and not afraid to use his blades, so the dog's entire body language is non-confrontational. Note the lifted paw, seal ears, tucked rear end and head dip. The dog's body language is screaming "no conflict please".

There is absolutely no aggression in this dog's communication at all. Often the dog will move away from the scary thing if he can and never show aggression. The exception to this is when escape is not possible, so the dog tries something else, of a more overt nature, that works and becomes a habit.

Resource guarding is a perfect example of natural overt behaviour. In this picture, despite being a young puppy the dog on the left is seriously guarding a food item. Look at his hard stare and full pucker. The dog on the right is wisely looking away to avoid conflict.

Here's another picture where one dog is intimidating the other via a hard stare and display of teeth. The second dog is not interested in conflict at all and is simply asking to be left alone.

If you see a dog acting like the one on the left in this picture it's vital to alleviate the tension and remove any other dog or person from their space. The antagonistic pucker can be a distance increasing signal and most of the time it is – however it can also be a prelude to a definite attack.

The dog on your right above is practicing submission. He may be a dog that practices submission regularly as that's his way of avoiding conflict. Rolling over with one paw in the air with an exposed belly is the dog's way of saying he's not wanting to fight. It's termed passive submission because the dog is not interested in appeasing or actively offering submissive behaviours – he's just passively hoping that the threat will go away.

Here's another example of passive submission, this time the dog that is inspecting is not showing an antagonistic pucker or particular tension, yet the puppy is taking no chances.

Submission is active or passive. The dog that chooses passive is likely to freeze, avoid eye contact and wait it out until the threat or trigger goes away. The dog that is trying to make friends and actively convince the other not to threaten him anymore is practicing active submission and often appeasement behaviour too.

The picture above shows common appeasement and active submission from a puppy to an older dog.

A dog may also use obnoxious submission which can be somewhat irritating for the recipient. Obnoxious submission is physical and right in the recipient's face. It will often be delivered via I insistent muzzle licking and rolling over, whilst simultaneously ignoring any distance increasing requests from the recipient. The dog who offers obnoxious submission is forcing their desperate need for affiliation on another by being both annoying and submissive at the same time.

Tension

If a dog does not naturally choose submission in a situation where conflict may arise, we can see the tension in their body language and general stance. A tense dog on greeting does not necessarily mean a fight will ensue, it could be based on nervousness, and communication may defuse the whole thing. Or the tension may become the prelude to an aggressive display or even an attack – it's all about the individuals.

Dogs may appear tense then generally defuse each other's approach by communicating perfectly, leading both dogs to becoming more relaxed. Or on a more sinister level tension may become a momentary freeze than attack. The body language leading up to relaxation or attack may initially begin by looking similar but as the dog's intention is becoming his behaviour, the body language will split and become very different.

If greeting tension is due to the dog not being sure, and yet not wanting to trigger or offer conflict and this dog is open to negotiation and alliance, they will head for the other dog's rear end, curve around and become more animated. For example, they may soften in the face, do little hops or a paw lift and even with a high tail they may begin to wag. Initially this dog may have appeared tense and quite scary, but communication has relieved how he feels so the dog is starting to relax and cope with the greeting.

In the picture these two dogs are greeting in the right body position, the black dog is looking intimidated which is unsurprising considering the stance of the second dog. However, the second dog is not directly staring, he's not looking at the first dog's face and is greeting with good manners. This situation could escalate but it's more likely that this is two unsure dogs greeting in the best way they know how. The brown and white dog in the picture above is showing that he's worried through hackles, tail height and facial tension but he's not threatening.

If the greeting goes the other way though, and one of the dogs is likely to be confrontational they will have a quiet confidence. The best way I can describe this is in a dog I met at the woods a while ago. My own Mr Chips is a defensive barker and scared of bigger dogs so when we saw a yellow Labrador coming the other way, we hid behind a tree to distract him and wait it out. Chips was on the lead and finding treats when the off lead Labrador came right into our space and breached his flight distance. Chips naturally started barking at the other dog to go away, by this point there was nowhere for us to go and he certainly couldn't be let off the lead as he would have believed his only choice was to fight – based on the space invasion.

The other dog's reaction was chilling. He held his space and was completely silent staring directly at Chips, totally confident with a barely audible throat growl. By this point he was completely frozen and seconds from launching into Chips. I put myself between the dogs and tried hard to distract the Labrador away. The dog's walker wandered up and said "he's OK" although the dog was far from ok but eventually we managed to get from behind our tree and continue our walk.

There's an instinctive response when we encounter a dog that truly means to do harm. Adrenaline floods our muscles and if they are focussed on one of our own dogs it's even worse. In my experience the silent, frozen, hard eyed dog is the real threat because they have the confidence to handle themselves, often based on learning how to in situations that distressed them, sometimes though just because they are competent. The loud barker, big aggressive display is often accompanied with fear signals showing us that this dog would rather be anywhere else.

Whilst most dogs prefer peace agreements every dog can bite in the right circumstances. Our job is to recognise how they feel and prevent them from escalating to that point, by changing the environment around them and not putting them into situations where they think it's necessary. Just like we are unlikely to instigate an argument when we are not stressed, relaxed dogs are not likely to react negatively to their environment and can cope better with potential triggers. If a dog feels stressed, is cornered or his communications are ignored, this dog is more likely to believe his only choice is aggression.

The Dog's Intention

Loosely speaking we can split aggression between fear based non-confrontational aggression or the dog that is confrontational and willing to follow though, with a physical attack.

A fearful dog isn't likely to bite a person or other animal unless he can't leave the situation. When this happens, he continues to cower but, at the same time shows his teeth and might growl or snarl. If he snaps or bites, it's usually quick, and then he retreats as far away from the threat as possible.

An exception to this is the dog who has learned that warning does not work. The ladder of aggression is based on a set of warning signs that finally become a bite. If any dog has tried to communicate the warning signs in the past, but they have been ignored, he may go straight to bite.

Confrontation

The aggression that is displayed when the dog is prepared for confrontation means that the dog is not showing fear behaviour. Remember though, that fear is likely to be the basis of this behaviour but over time it may have been replaced with a confidence, usually because polite requests have been previously ignored.

Confrontational aggression shows specific body language, this dog may be dictating to the trigger that they have a chance to retreat. He is likely to show the following signs:

- Ears up and forward.
- Growls, snarls or barks in a low, threatening tone.
- Hackles may be up.
- May look large and intimidating by holding his head high.
- Positions himself over his forelegs so that he's ready to lunge or charge forward.
- Teeth are displayed.
- Stares directly at the person or animal.
- Tail raised and rigid.

Much like the Labrador I described earlier in this chapter.

With canine aggression every case is unique, there is no one size fits all reason or treatment. In some cases, aggression is fear driven, carried out because the dog feels he has no choice or seemingly spontaneous. Dogs who have suffered physical abuse can seem to display aggression without warning. This can be due to being punished for giving warning signals such as growling or lip raising, in the past. Dog aggression naturally escalates from early warning signals to attack mode, if one of those steps has been punished it tends not to be repeated.

Often a dog will seem to be aggressive towards other dogs when really, he is not thinking of fighting at all, he just doesn't know what else to do.

Aggression towards people can be caused by fear, usually fear of the person that the aggression is aimed towards. It could also be general fear of the situation which the dog is dealing with at the time. An example is a dog in kennels that shows his teeth through the bars because he's scared and confused. Another example is guarding the house for fear of the dangerous stranger that may enter it.

Fear and Non-confrontation

Defusing aggression is a matter of careful communication. If two dogs are showing aggressive behaviour to each other, increasing the distance between them should defuse the tension, preventing any escalation.

The next step would be to teach the dogs that the presence of the other animal is a rewarding and relaxing experience. This can be done with counter conditioning and careful desensitisation. The dogs should be side by side, rewarded when they are relaxed and only bought closer together as a careful process of relaxation, reward and subsequent distance decrease. At the moment that any anxiety is shown the distance between the dogs should be increased.

If a dog is aggressive towards a human, then it's important to give the animal space and communicate in a way that he understands. Calming signals should be used and there should be no behaviour that the dog can see as confrontation. As much as possible the dog should be left alone and certainly not forced into any interaction.

Dog and human reassurance is very different, when a human reassures and tries to make friends a dog may see threat and confrontation. We need to talk in dog language to a scared dog, as much as we can. We can use calming signals is the way that dogs do.

Fear aggression is often seen when a scared dog is cornered. Dealing with a fearful dog is about recognising what exactly causes the fear and the distance where the anxiety begins. The most important thing to remember is that fear behaviour should never be punished because it will make the fear worse.

To gain the trust of a scared dog is amazing. It's earned by acting in a way that shows the scared dog you are no threat. For example, if the dog is showing mild calming signals towards you it is beneficial to respond in a language that he will understand. By doing this you will be showing him that you are no threat. Eye contact should always be avoided.

A scared dog will see direct approach as confrontation and this position will not help him to cope. Many people talk to a worried dog and look them in the eye, as they would a worried person, but that's the worst thing to do in this kind of situation. To help a worried dog to cope you can offer calming signals back to him and simultaneously mirror his behaviour. A scared aggressive dog will benefit from the following respectful treatment.

- Respect the dog's personal space, remember flight distance and critical distance. Touching a scared dog will scare him more. Allow him to decompress in his own time.

- Allow the dog to come to you and do not force physical contact on him. With very scared dogs this can take a little while but is building trust between the dog and you so it's worth that few extra minutes.

- If the dog becomes more persistent with his calming signals or begins to growl or snap, then you are moving too quickly for him. If possible in this situation it is better to leave and try again later even just sit at the distance where he can settle for a while. Being near but not in his personal space is allowing him to get used to your presence in his own time.

Aggression is easy to recognise when you know what to look for. It starts with a single glance and follows right through to a bite. Only the most socially adept dog will follow the process though for each step to be recognisable. Many have their own style in the road to a bite, some may miss entire steps as they have previously been ignored and go straight for the bite.

A dog's body language will usually change in at least some notable way before he becomes aggressive. The process from fear to bite will be similar to this:

- The dog will focus on the trigger (the thing that he's worried about) this may be very brief.

- Calming signals will follow, the dog may glance away, yawn or try to leave the situation.

- If the calming signals do not take away the trigger the dog will then change his posture, shift his bodyweight, his hackles may raise, and he may growl.
- If growling doesn't work the dog will show his teeth.
- If flashing the teeth doesn't work, he may snap at the air between him and the trigger
- The next thing that may occur in these the dog may freeze, this is a very brief act and can be missed if you're not looking for it. The freeze is the dog making a decision to either fight or flee the threat.
- If he can't leave the situation or the stimulant is not removed the dog is at severe risk of biting. This is because he feels he has no choice and his warnings are not working.

Some dogs, as an exception to the above, have learned to cope so well with their fears that they don't even show that they're scared or uncomfortable before the aggression manifests. This is because this reaction has been used by the dog for so long that he relies on it as a default response to something he sees as a threat.

Takeaway Points

- Aggression is a natural behaviour, yet most dogs won't choose to be aggressive.
- The way that a dog acts when they become aggressive will depend on their intention.
- There are many reasons for aggression and the vet should always be consulted in the case of sudden onset aggression.
- All dogs showing aggression should be given space in the first instance.
- Tension on greeting can lead to affiliation or attack depending on both parties and how they handle the situation.
- A fearful dog can learn to trust if treated with respect and allowed to heal in their own time.
- Our biggest tools when understanding dogs are our eyes and our education. Using Enlightened Observation.

Summary

I really hope you have enjoyed the book and learned a lot about the dogs you spend time with. Dogs are amazing, we have spent generations barely listening to them, yet they have adapted and remained our constant companions throughout.

If you are in any doubt about how your dog is feeling, take a moment and watch him carefully. If you don't understand his communication or why he uses certain signals together or in specific situations, make it your challenge to research that. It's a wonderful world to share with dogs, it's even better when our conversations with them are two-way and accurate.

Thank you for reading.

Final Note

If you're reading this through kindle please could you click the star rating at the end of the book. Reviews and ratings are the lifeblood of self-published authors. Reviews dictate readers, readers mean better understood dogs and happier guardians. They also get this work seen by as many people as possible, so I would really appreciate it if you took a moment just to click to share your experience.

If you have found the subject interesting please do take a look at the Canine Communication Diploma course provided by Canine Principles, I wrote that and Dayle Smith Illustrated it. The Diploma extremely detailed plus an accredited course for professionals and anyone that wants to learn more.

Thank you for joining me.

If you have any questions or just want to say hello, you can contact me at my website sallygutteridge.com and I respond to every single message.

Enjoy your dogs!

Index

Printed in Great Britain
by Amazon